Extrapolating
the Unknown

Extrapolating the Unknown

A Unified View on Spirituality

M. V. K. Mohan

PARTRIDGE

Library of Congress Control Number:		2017952897
ISBN:	Softcover	978-1-5437-4141-4
	eBook	978-1-5437-4142-1

Print information available on the last page.

To order additional copies of this book, contact
Toll Free 800 101 2657 (Singapore)
Toll Free 1 800 81 7340 (Malaysia)
orders.singapore@partridgepublishing.com

www.partridgepublishing.com/singapore

Contents

Introduction ix

The Law of Correspondence 1

    The Law Illustrated by More Examples 5

    Extrapolating Upwards and Downwards 7

The Phenomenon of Alternating Virtual Reality 8

    The Phenomenon of Multiple Life Forms in the Same System ... 10

    Is It Possible to Have a Level 1.5? 11

    Life Defined 12

        Life Defined from a Higher Viewpoint 13

        Life Defined from the Same-Level Viewpoint 14

    Are Countries Living Things? What about Rivers and
    Mountains? 19

How to Find Out If a System Is Living 22

The Law As It Is Applied to the Physical Plane 25

The Law As Applied to the Mental Plane 26

    Understanding the Mind by Understanding the World 32

    The Commonality in All Levels 36

Correspondence Between Dreams and Our Real World 37

Correspondence Between Diseases and the Mental Plane 41

The Law as It Is Applied to the Spiritual Plane 43

Our Relationship to God 43

What Is Death? What Happens When We Die? 44

Our Own Death Is Not Possible 47

Is Rebirth Possible? 48

Do Ghosts Exist? 50

What Is Time? Is It Absolute or Relative? How Is It Created? 52

Parallel Universes, Different Time Speeds 56

How Would God Look Upon Us or Feel About Us? 57

Corollary 1: Even God Has Problems Managing Us! 58

Corollary 2: God Really Does Not Care for Each One
of Us as Long as the Theme Is Continuing 59

Corollary 3: God Will Be Aware of Us Only if Forced To ...59

Attracting God's Attention 60

What Is My Dharma (My Duty, My Calling)? 62

Fate and Self-Effort 65

What Is My Karma (fate)? 65

Why Are These Things Happening to Me? How Do I
Change Them? 68

Why Is Desire So Good? 69

Energy Flow Is the Most Enjoyable Thing 73

Why Do We Need New Movies Every Year? Why Is Stereo Sound So Good? 76

Why Do We Laugh? Why Are Jokes Funny? 77

Male and Female Energies 79

The Law as Applied to Meditation 81

Why and How Meditation Works 82

What Is Meditation? 84

Magnetism and Magnetic Personalities 90

What Is It That We Are Really After? How Do We Get It? Mantra Chanting 93

How to Meditate 96

The Law Applied to Moksha, or Enlightenment 101

What Is Moksha? 101

What Is Enlightenment? 104

How Do We Achieve It? 104

Methodology of Shaktipath, Kundalini Yoga, and Similar Traditions 106

Renunciation 109

Applying All of This Theory 113

Some Miscellaneous Topics 120

How the Universe Was Made 120

Is It Right to Kill Others? Is It Ever Justifiable? 121

Is It Right to Kill Ourselves? 123

Is the Majority Always Right? 124

Unanswered Questions 125

Bibliography 127

Introduction

The ideas in this book have been within me for a long time, but I did not put them in writing as I always felt that there was something missing. However, as the concepts are so profound, I felt that to wait for perfection may be futile. And even if I did fully understand the concepts one day, I am not sure I would be able write from the same level of awareness at that time that I am in right now. Who knows? I might not feel the need for writing the obvious.

I was always struck by the way difficult concepts are so often explained by examples in seemingly unrelated fields. The only caution authors often give is that we should not extend the example too much. One day I came across the hermetic law that formally declares that similarities are the order in the world. I started to look for places or phenomena in which it does not exist, but I could see only more and more proof that it does exist. The Law of Correspondence, like the Law of Energy, cannot be proved; it can only be illustrated that it always exists. The law, when applied, states that the level seen above and the level unseen below are the same phenomenon or processes. I applied it further. If you want to see how one level above us would look, or one level below, observe whichever level we can observe and extrapolate what happens at the other level.

Then I started thinking about the practical use of this theory. Would the Law of Correspondence make our lives better in any way? How do we make use of this principle? Once we accept its existence, it could be used as a tool to probe concepts that cannot be experienced or understood. For example, is there a god? If there is, how does this god feel? Why is he seemingly partial to a few? How do we define life? Am *I* living or are my cells are living—or both? Is life continuous or discrete? Can this law be used to improve our health? What is meditation, and why and how must we meditate? Will taking a different view of life, a different view of God, help us in any way? How do we make life better for ourselves, for society? Some ideas emerged.

Then my thoughts went to abstract concepts like nirvana. What I had read was all theory, and I was able to get an intellectual feel for it. If a thorough understanding could lead us to nirvana, the next question anyone would ask is, then why don't you check it out yourself before you come out with the book? As I said before, maybe then I would not ever write the book.

Maybe none of the thoughts mentioned here are new to the world; maybe someone somewhere has already elaborated upon them in a better manner. After all, the law is not new, I am only elaborating on it. But the application of the principles and the topics presented here are my own.

Along the way many doubts emerged whether I was stretching the concepts too much. Maybe the law can be applied only to a few situations, though nowhere did I see any conditions attached to the law. I have introduced a section in the last for unanswered questions on correspondence. The list is changing even as I write the book; maybe others can resolve or comment on those later.

These concepts are found in books written in the previous century and even by current spiritual leaders. For example, in a book by Geoffrey Hodson,1986 in *Meditations on the Occult Life*, writes:

> Life at any point or in any part of the solar system, is an epitome of the whole. The evolution of the group consciousness of mineral, plant, animal, and nature-spirit into angelhood and of animal into humanity is a microcosmic reflection of a macrocosmic achievement .... In the study of the spiritual, this

principle should be applied. Without it all knowledge is as the shell which hides the kernel of the fruit of the tree of life. Therefore, the occult student should meditate upon unity until a measure of experience of the whole has been attained. From experience of the interior essential fact, he may then proceed to study with comprehension the external and relatively unessential parts of the whole. True interpretation demands synthetic thought based upon the understanding of the whole …. In the darkness of universal night the solar worlds are born. In the darkness of the earth, the germination of the seed occurs and plants are born. In the darkness of a mother's womb the body of a child is formed. From absolute darkness, suns, globes, plants and men emerge into the light. ….

…That principle which was the flower in the plant is expressed as the head of the animal, that which was the roots is now symbolized by the feet – still attached to earth, but mobile…. The head of the animal thrust forth from the body reflects in microcosmic form the existence of extra-systemic consciousness and life. It corresponds to the apex of the pyramid, the valve through which the life which is beyond is enabled to reach the life already within…

…Non-manifestation is the higher essence of existence and is in no sense separate from the manifest….. This is true of all kingdoms of life.

In this book he also quotes books by Dr. Annie Besant. He writes that the macrocosm and the microcosm exhibit the same properties. He also says in another chapter that crystals are forms of life in the mineral world.

Taken with other Vedic statements like *Purnamidam Purnascha*, which means that the part is nothing but the whole, this hermetic law seems to have a sound base. Similarly the vedic statement *"Yatha Pinde*

Thata Brahmande, which means that, as is the atom, so is the universe. After all, if we are a part of the whole, then would we not have the same properties of the whole and vice versa?

Aditya Hridayam, is a hymn for invoking the sun god. This can be seen from three different planes. One plane is that sun is a god, and he gives us everything we know. Second is that there is a higher god, and he is seen through the sun, thus sun is just a portal through which all other gods like Shiva, Vishnu, and Devi shine. The third plane is that whatever is shining in the sun god is also shining through me; in essence, I am made up of the same stuff as the sun god.

The theory of the chakras, the energy centres in the body is well known. There are seven chakras in the human body. The *Muladhara* (the chakra situated at the base of the spine) is the chakra of memory, egoism, materialism, and dominance. The next chakra is *Svadhishtana (the chakra situated just below the navel),* and it deals with reason and intellect. The next chakra is *Manipura (the chakra at the solar plexus).* This chakra can direct human will either to the lower chakras of ego, reasoning, and dominance, or to the higher chakras of the heart. The next chakra is of the *Anahata* (chakra situated at the heart level) and awakens love and intuition. Intuition is not against reason, but only much quicker in arriving at the same result. It seems the human lives in the first chakra from birth till seven years of age. During this time the child strives to control and know his or her body and know which things to go after and which to be afraid of. Between seven fourteen years of age, the child is keen to know the what and the why of everything; he or she strives to reason out everything. Next, as a teenager, the child asserts his or her will and does not listen to anyone else. If the person progresses after this, over the next seven years, though cognizant of the above things, he or she develops a tolerance and understanding of society and loves nature in general. My point in mentioning this is not to give a lecture on the chakras, but to point out correspondence at various levels. There are seven chakras and there are seven tones in the musical scale. It is said that each tone activates a particular chakra and certain songs which concentrate on particular notes have the capacity to affect us because the note affects the chakra and hence our emotions. Similarly, there are seven colours in the rainbow, memorized as VIBGYOR. Each colour is also associated with each chakra and is supposed to affect our moods by affecting the chakra. What is most interesting is the similarity with the evolution of society. In the beginning, we find members of society trying to overcome fears and obsessed with the basic instincts, trying to dominate nature and other tribes. This corresponds to the *Muladhara* chakra, the first in the evolution of mankind. Then comes the age of the Greeks who asserted reason, ordering and categorizing knowledge with debates. This corresponds to the *Svadishtana* chakra. Next a society develops a "will" and developed science, weapons, and countries. It is believed that, in the present time, nations are more or less built, and we are in the age corresponding to the *anahata* or universal love. We understand war and other such things, but someone comes along and brokers peace. So the development of humanity is shown to follow what is inherent in the structure of humanity, thus proving again that what is inside is what is outside. From my observation, newly formed countries behave like toddlers; they are driven by animal instincts and are afraid of everything. Teenage countries behave like teenagers do, wanting to control everything and everybody; they are prepared for a fight anytime. Older countries have a huge tolerance for everything. The animals live amongst the people, almost anything is tolerated. It is like an old man who has seen everything and who wonders about the point of it all.

Though we keep seeing examples of the law in daily life, great thinkers who used this principle gave a boost to my confidence about my book. In fact, many people apply this law without even questioning its validity because it is so deeply ingrained into our thinking.

The assumptions we make about our environment, life and ourselves are tested only by a few extreme cases. It is these extreme cases we need to investigate to gain the correct knowledge. Even today, for most cases, we can go with the assumption that the earth is flat. The way people started questioning this belief is interesting. There was one case which could not be answered by the assumption of a flat earth. When we look at an approaching ship from the shore, the mast is seen first, then the bottom part of the ship. If the earth was flat, we should have seen the whole ship at once is it not? This and other such cases led to questioning the belief of a flat earth and even calculated the radius of the earth only by extrapolation. Similarly, if we know that whatever we are aware of, we are not that, for example we are aware of the car, so we are not the car. Similarly, we are aware of our body, so we are not the body. We are aware of our mind and its thoughts, so we are not the mind either. Then what are we? Should we be worried about what happens to thing which are not us?

It may appear that I have given a very shallow treatment of profound topics, or that I have painted the topics with a broad brush. This could be true to some extent, and maybe a more detailed analysis is required on some topics. It would also require some sort of validation of the theories. If there is interest on this line of thinking, maybe I could expand upon my ideas in a second edition.

But if I meet with some success, would I ever be motivated to write a second book? Would a king who is dreaming of losing a war with an enemy king, upon waking up, go back to the dream and crush the enemy? Or would he just move on in the waking state? If we are in the dream of a higher entity, would we, after switching to the higher plane, walk away from this world or come back to write a book? My wife suggested I at least record my thoughts as they come up, as I was even forgetting the line of thought. Another thing is that I will never get the same set of thoughts because thought is always dynamic. I may get more clarity or may even scrap the whole idea of writing a book. Writing in this confused mindset full of thoughts may be a good thing in case some readers may also have the same doubts. Carl Sagan, the great astronomer, advised to always have a pencil and notebook ready to write down any ideas that come about. It seems that a thought is the crystallization of a variety of internal and external factors, so it is impossible to get the same thought more than once. Hence I look at this book as a recording of my thoughts while I am in my current state.

In one of my discussions with my Guru, he advised me to record my ideas, as in the least, it is a *kriya* (a manifestation of creative thoughts and deeds) that I must share. As a true *Karma Yogi* (one who does action for the sake of purification of oneself, not for the fruits of action), I am supposed to come out with the book and not worry about the results. That is why I have come out with my thoughts on paper.

At best, this book should be seen as a work in progress. Maybe someone will take off on this tool and elaborate other concepts better than I have done.

The Law of Correspondence

The hermetic Law of Correspondence states: "As above so below; as below so above; as within so without; as without so within."

This law tells us that things which appear to be very different have attributes that are actually quite similar. It also tells us that by studying one thing we can learn about something else.

It is said that an effect is nothing but a cause in another form; for example, a gold ornament is nothing but gold in another form.

It is very difficult to prove this law, just as we cannot really prove the Law of Conservation of Energy. The Law of Conservation of Energy rests solely on the argument that it has not been disproved, but has been observed everywhere to be true.

However, some Vedic statements like *Purnamidam Purnascha*, (which says that the part is nothing but the whole and if you remove a part, the whole remains), lends weight to the hermetic law. In ancient vedic texts, it is written that all things in this world, living and non living things are made up of the five elements in various proportions of the five elements, space, air, fire, water, earth (like 1/12 air, 1/32 water, etc). So if we are nothing but the part of a whole (and so are members of the plant kingdom, and so is the solar system), then is it not logical to think that correspondence exists? After all, we are all parts of the same thing.

As I am basing the whole book on Law of Correspondence, most readers would want an elaborate proof of a new theory, but unfortunately, this section is going to be a small one. It is based, as is the Law of Conservation of Energy, on observation of facts. I don't think there is any example which goes against the law of conservation of energy. Similarly is the case with the Law of correspondence. Later, the observation that the virtual and real worlds alternate and are purely virtual or real based on point of view is verifiable by experience. In short, I cannot offer any proof, but by observing the phenomenon that I elaborate upon you might arrive at the same conclusion.

Neither is this law my own theory; I present only some observations, elaborations, and conclusions. If we can improve our world based on these observations and inferences, it would be a bonus.

The Law of Correspondence can be useful. For example, when we cannot know the reality or behaviour of some thing or place, we can look either upward or downward (or inward or outward), to a dimension to which we have access or understanding, and draw conclusions from what we observe.

Whenever we try to explain something, we take an example. The example is something that we understand well; hence, we will understand the new concept too. The principle under operation is the Law of Correspondence. (Care should be taken to see that extraneous factors should not make the example incorrect. However, as in all phenomena, when all variables are known, things become understandable.)

I once saw an article about the way a leaf looks when magnified. First, the leaf is a small part of the tree, and the tree is seen as the living entity. However, upon magnification, the terrain of the leaf looks similar to a forest, with a network of rivers where fluids flow. We see undulations that remind us of mountains and other land formations. Hence, we could say that it is the leaf that is actually the living thing, and the tree is just a complex of leaves. On further magnification, we see that the leaves are actually composed of cells, and these are actually the living things. Different types of cells exist, and because they all seem to work in a precise and mutually helpful way, they seem to form a system.

So, the tree or the leaf no longer seems to be the entity; the cells seem to be the living things, and a leaf or a tree is a collection of cells. On further magnification, the cells seem to be mere placeholders; the actual elements of the cell are the living things. There is the nucleus, which is the core, a mitochondrion, which breathes, scavengers, and circulatory systems, and so forth, which make up a complete system. We magnify further and see that the cell bodies are themselves nothing but atoms and molecules. We see that DNA is a certain arrangement of proteins. We magnify further to see that each atom has a nucleus, and electrons whiz around the nucleus just as the planets whiz around the Sun. We don't have a method to magnify further, so we move back to the leaf. The leaf forms a part of a tree. Zooming up, we see that the tree is a part of a forest, and the tree itself looks to be part of the forest. The terrain of the forest is similar to what we saw in the leaf. We zoom up further to see the earth. Actually, each tree and each animal looks like a cell doing its precise work to maintain the system. The earth, from a far distance, looks like the electron zooming around the sun, the nucleus. Extending further, the sun seems part of a galaxy, and so forth. I saw a NASA video of a star gobbling up planets. I am sure if someone took a photo of cells ingesting food particles, it would look the same. So would two atoms fighting for an electron. As above (planets and galaxies), so below (electrons and atoms). There is also a video I saw about how the cells and atoms in our body correspond to the world, then to stars, and finally to galaxies.

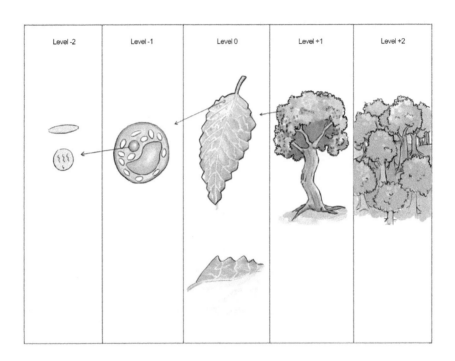

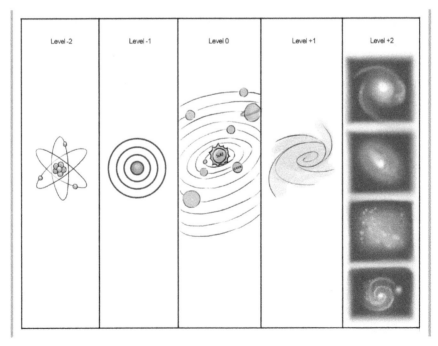

There are two observations I would like to highlight. First, there is a similarity between the smallest thing and the largest; for example, the way electrons seem to be whizzing around a nucleus, which is similar to planets going around the sun. A galaxy is similar to any mass of commonly seen matter. This pattern repeats at higher and lower levels. Second, there is something we call life, but what appears to be the living thing from one point of view (the leaf) is actually part of a tree (the higher level) and at the lower level of the leaf, the cells seem to be the real living things. The alternate views of what is living extend both up and down as far as we can observe.

The Law of Correspondence paints with a very broad brush. It cannot, for example, predict if it will rain tomorrow. In this way, it is similar to the Law of Conservation of Energy. Though the Law of Conservation of Energy is true, it had been misinterpreted to mean that all moving things come to a rest of their own, and it requires a force to keep things moving. It was necessary for Newton to disprove it, and now Newton's laws are common knowledge.

The Law Illustrated by More Examples

We will see more examples in future chapters, but the important ones are the parallels between the dreaming state and the waking state.

The *Mudakopanishad (Upanishads are sacred texts found in the vedas and Mundakopanishad is one of them)* is a detailed analysis of the waking and the dream state and concludes that both are unreal. Both states have striking similarities, and any differences we see are due to a number of faculties and instruments that are different; for example, in the dream state we don't use the physical body, and in that sense we feel it is not real. For the purposes of illustrating the Law of Correspondence, we see that both states have an observer – the individual "I" or the ego – and in both states we experience feelings and enact reactions to what we observe. The body is an extra instrument available during the waking state, but otherwise the thoughts, feelings, fears, and worries are all the same. In fact many concepts we see during the dream and waking states are the same, and the worries of the day play out during dreams too. This is true of any joys and achievements during the day which are constantly replayed for our benefit and enjoyment.

Another important parallel is the one between our thought world and our waking world. In both of these states, again, the observer – *I*, the ego, – is present. Thoughts are equivalent to the living things we see in the real word. Almost always, thoughts are born out of other thoughts. All thoughts are combinations of other thoughts, just as experiences in the real world are combinations of other experiences. This is similar to the world where we observe that all living things where born out of some other living thing. Which came first, the chicken or the egg? This question is like, which thought came first? Supposing you like an apple? How did you know it was an apple? What is the meaning of "like". When someone described the apple they used that it was similar to something you knew. If you knew nothing, it is impossible to explain anything. The new knowledge gained becomes the block on which other words and thoughts are built. But what was the first thought? If we go back in our thought process, we must go to the idea that "initially there was the word" type of a statement found in religious texts.

Thoughts are born with some energy and want to live forever, just like living things we see in daily life. Their energy is the attention we give them. Thoughts will do anything to survive and frequently feed off the energy of other thoughts. All politics we see in the external world happen in our thought world. Birds of a feather flock together in life similarly to the way similar thoughts hang out with each other. Misery loves company in both worlds. On a sad note, just as we are not in control of the real world, we don't have much control over our thoughts either. Most of us are just capable of initiating thoughts; after that we helplessly watch them take over our mental world. We make feeble attempts to control our thoughts by introducing other thoughts, but we are not actually sure how to kill the old thoughts. Thoughts behave just like living things. Perhaps the most striking similarity is that in both the worlds, there is an "I" who is the observer, who feels that he or she is the doer. I will elaborate on this later in this book.

As inside, so outside.

I will be drawing heavily on this concept when we discuss meditation and other topics.

Extrapolating Upwards and Downwards

Let us go back to the example of the leaf. Let's look at the forest, which is made up of trees. We believe the trees are the real living things, which would mean that the forest is the virtual reality. Just as the tree is a living thing, can we say that the forest is living? What is the relationship between a forest and its trees? To answer that, we could look downwards and ask what the relationship of the leaves to the tree is. Just as a tree is a virtual being, which is a delicate system, present only until the balance between all the leaves and their loyalty exists, we could see the forest as a system in balance with all its constituents – trees, plants, water, and air. Could there be things in the forest that don't belong to the forest? Yes, take for example, the billion bacterial cells in our bodies that are not part of us as people. Similarly we could point out several living entities that might exist within the living entity of the forest, but that are not the forest; for example we might find men and animals in the forest. Even a collection of creepers among the trees could be termed another life and so on. So we could have a multitude of systems all existing within the same physical entity. The important point here is how we define life and how our awareness assumes that a certain system is one. We will elaborate later.

The Phenomenon of Alternating Virtual Reality

There is a pattern of alternating real and virtual entities. Which do we say is real – the cell or the leaf or the tree?

All the cells that define me, Mohan the individual, are living; they are actually "me". The number of bacteria and other cellular organisms in our bodies outnumber our own cells 10:1 (commonly believed to be the case and 1:1 by some latest research). It seems there are four broad types of bacteria such as those found in the mouth, the anus, the vagina, and on the skin. Some of these are called good bacteria because, without them, many diseases and conditions like asthma could prevail. So there are many more cells in my body than those that make up "me", like unwanted bacteria, which I don't consider part of myself. So I would define myself as those cells that are loyal to the concept of an entity called Mohan and would act as desired by Mohan. If you ask my cells who Mohan is, they would not know, never mind what he does or wants. All that they might infer is that there is some higher-level entity that is organizing the whole system, and magically all things seem to be working like clockwork.

Another point is that the virtual entity is seen as the god by the lower entity; whereas in actual fact, the higher level really depends upon the absolute loyalty of all the lower-level entities. Unless each and every cell is loyal and does the work it is supposed to, Mohan cannot live. If suddenly a group of cells breaks out feeling that they are better off fending for themselves, they are seen as cancer. Similarly, unless all the citizens of a country live and work together, the country breaks up.

The higher-level entity, while dependent on the loyalty of the lower levels, is actually worried about issues that the lower level can never ever understand. For example, how would I explain to each and every cell that it is OK for me to shave off my facial hair in order to look good to other living things? I can never explain to my cells why it is important to have money in the bank. In fact, there is no means of communication between my cells and myself. I just have to know what they want and keep providing it in exchange for unquestioned loyalty to the concept called me.

Similarly, the higher-level entity (me) is actually not very worried about what happens to a few cells as long as the whole system is maintained. Sometimes I am even OK sacrificing a few cells for some other benefit which cannot be explained to the cells or organs below. In fact, I might even ask them to endure more pain for a higher cause. Suppose my thigh muscles complain that they are aching and they need rest. But I see that a dog is chasing me. I would urge my muscles to run harder in spite of their complaint. I can never explain to the leg muscles why they are asked to work more at that time.

Another sobering fact is that I am not actually aware of what the cells want unless they actually communicate, and they do so through pain and pleasure. When there is a problem with the cells, I always send medicine or some other therapy that will ensure order again. (In the *Bhagavad Gita* we read that God will interfere whenever there is chaos and break down of systems.) Actually it is in my own interest that I keep the system in harmony for my own survival. The only catch is that the approach taken should be broad rather than based on individual cells. That is to say, I will not worry too much about one cell, but about a group of cells or an organ. While each and every cell is me, I do not worry if a few cells go away or are replaced. It all depends on the situation at that moment. However, when a group of cells have a problem – say, for example, an organ has a problem – I get worried and start to act.

Let us project upwards. We are the lower-level reality of a higher-level entity we call God. Will we ever understand why the higher-level reality is doing things the way he is? No. This can be compared to the fact that our cells cannot understand us: we can never understand God or why he does what he does. Will the higher level (God?) ever look at things at a cell-by-cell level? Maybe, and maybe not. It depends on the communication (pain or pleasure for instance). When we have a problem, will the higher reality help us? Absolutely, and more so when it is in his own interest. What should we do? Just do what we are supposed to do to our best ability and be loyal to the entire creation as we see it. This is just the way we want our cells to be. Actually, God himself could have a higher entity. If he did, he might be worried about how to attract his higher reality's attention. In our *puranas* (Hindu sacred texts), every god including the trinity has a higher god.

Another thing: if we want more attention and energy from God and we want him to help us, the only way is to identify what is relevant to him and fulfil that to the best of our extent. When we are relevant, God will extend all help to see that we live better. In comparison, I would take more care of my legs if I needed them to be in top working condition. I will elaborate on this topic in the section called "What Is My Dharma (my duty)?".

The Phenomenon of Multiple Life Forms in the Same System

Let us continue to use the example of our body. As mentioned before, our bodies are made of many trillion cells. Studies show that almost half of them are cells we call our "own". The rest are cells that reside in our body but are for the most part "good bacteria" and a few which are inimical to us. There is actually a full-scale war going on most of the time within our bodies between the cells that owe allegiance to us and those that don't. So, do we say that *I*, as a human being, exist? Or do we say that a human is a virtual reality made up of individual real entities, which are the cells? Or do we say that the cell components are real, like the nucleus and mitochondria, and that the cells are virtual?

We observe that reality and virtual entities alternate. Indeed, which is virtual or real is purely dependent on the observer's viewpoint.

I can look at my body and say that the cells make up the organs and the organs, like the heart and the liver, are actually living things, and Mohan is made up of these living things. So then, are the cells the real entity or the organs the real entity? Or is Mohan the real entity? It depends on who is asking.

So, it is possible that, in one system, different lives are living either independently or one above the other.

Extrapolating in another direction upwards, what is a country? A company? What are rivers and mountains? These are all sets of living things that form systems. Now I am not sure if consciousness exists in these things, but we do see proof of them reacting to their environment. So we can look at a country as a living thing. The country demands all its citizens owe complete allegiance to the country and its rules to survive. In return, the citizens expect their needs to be taken care of. So we could have in the same physical location, a company, a country, and the earth forming living things in their own right. Many country wide events we observe, like Independence Day, the national anthems, sports events, all are important from the country point of view. These rituals serve to unite the constituents of the living thing called the "Country" and this living entity reacts with its peers in defined ways.

Is It Possible to Have a Level 1.5?

I once read somewhere that some advanced sages could see the energy levels we are in currently, as well as a higher, shiny level above. Most souls were stuck to the current level, and suddenly some would actually jump to the next level. There would be no slow-motion movement from one level to the other. It was either this level or that level. This is similar to the energy or spin of electrons; they are either at one level or the other, never caught in between. This is also similar to the waking and dream states; either we are awake or asleep. So consciousness, identifying with a system that we can call life, will either be associated with one system or the other, never both systems. This is what gives individuality to the experience that creates what is called individual or ego.

I mentioned in the example of our body that the cells are on one level and we are at a higher level. But we could also think of the organs as another level in between. Hence, between a level 1 and a level 2, a level 1.5 is possible. For example, the heart and the liver could be living things, if we think of ourselves as made up of organs rather than cells.

Similarly, it is possible to think of "the god" and many levels below it. So it is perfectly logical that we think of a supreme god, and one level below who in total make up the supreme god and so on until we refer to our level, just as the ecosystem of the river can be construed as the river god and the ecosystem of the mountain can be construed as the mountain god. The mountain god would then comprise of all the plants, trees, and animals living on the mountain, and if the ecosystem is in balance, it can be termed logical that there is a living entity called a mountain. After all, is it not similar to us calling ourselves human, when actually we are just a collection of living cells? Hence it is perfectly possible for a wind god *Vayu*, for a rain god *Varuna*, and even their god called *Indra*.

In this sense, it would be perfectly logical if life assumed a set of living things and called itself a mountain, thus making a mountain a living thing. Now once it is a living thing, it will behave exactly as a living thing does. It will encourage those who support it, kill those who don't, and in general try to live as long as possible. At a higher level, the earth itself may be seen as a living thing comprising of all living things below it. I have elaborated elsewhere how some countries have declared rivers and nature as living entities.

Life Defined

A famous scientist once posed a conundrum which I believe has no real answer yet. The question is something like this: Suppose we create a computer that can think and talk just like a human being. A human being and the computer are both behind a screen. We pose a set of questions and we get the answers from both. How do we identify which one is a living being? If we cannot identify which one is the human, can we say both are living? How do we make out in real life which is a human and which is a robot? In fact, in the Star Trek series, there is a robot who looks like a human. Is he also living? What is the definition of life by which we can say who is living and who is simulated?

So, the question is, how do we identify if a thing is living? How do we define life?

Life Defined from a Higher Viewpoint

It all depends on who is asking the question to whom. In the phenomenon of alternating virtual reality, even life is alternating. What appears to be living in one level seems virtual to the other. Let me elaborate.

Consider my dream state. If one of the dream characters starts to wonder who he is, or wonders if anyone is living other than himself, or asks the "sleeper" whether the table in the dream is living or the tiger in the dream is living, what would my answer be? The question itself is wrong! All the things in the dream are equally living or dead! Yes, some are animated, some are dull and inert, but all are my dream only. The mountains in the dream are made up of the same components as the trees or the elephants in it. They are all one thing, and I enliven all of the dream. To say one thing is different from the other in any way, not only living or dead, makes no sense to me at all. If the character still persists and says that the living things in the dream act in a particular way, like eating, breathing and moving, while the rock does not, my answer would be that is because I directed it that way in my dream. I could have easily reversed the case and made the rocks fly or talk. So all are equally alive. Yes, some are more animated because of my attention on them, but otherwise all are the same.

Consider another example. My heart starts wondering if it is the only organ that is alive. Are the stomach and lungs alive? My reply to this would be to ask the heart to stop worrying about such things and continue its work! I mean, all organs are equally alive. The question is itself wrong; please continue your duties.

So from a higher viewpoint, the answer is simple: The question itself is wrong and all below are virtual, and I alone pervade the lower level, and all components of me are equally alive.

However, my higher-level awareness will think the same about me and hence the logic extends all the way to the top where there is only one thing. All things below are virtual. This is another way of characterizing the entire world as *maya,* or unreal.

Life Defined from the Same-Level Viewpoint

The question, however, is not so easy from the same-level point of view. Suppose I ask these questions: Is the fellow sitting next to me alive? How about the table? How about the robot trained to act like a man?

Since the question itself is wrong, the answer will be very difficult and long. Finally, at some stage we have to give up and point to the explanation in the previous section: all things are equally living or dead. But there is a reason that we need to answer a wrong question to get right results. In chemistry, for example, we are taught initially that there are many molecules and that actually water (H_2O) is made of a combination of hydrogen and oxygen atoms. Then we are told that, various chemical compounds with various properties are made of atoms. Then later we are told that atoms are made up of protons, neutrons, and electrons. Then why did we waste time reading about atoms? Finally, we learn there are particles known as bosons, quarks, and leptons. Is all our learning a waste then? No. It is possible to live with a wrong idea, as long as we are careful to draw the right interpretations. This helps us tremendously in explaining certain phenomena. Treating water as a molecule helps us explain the properties of water, but treating water as a collection of atoms helps us explain how hydrogen and oxygen combine to make water. When we need to explain nuclear explosions, we need to talk about the subatomic particles (protons, neutrons, and electrons). So when the limit of the concept is reached, we have to go back to the original construct.

I will try to define life from the same-level perspective, and when we can no longer hold the concept, I will get back to the original claim that the question itself was wrong.

From the previous section, we know that there is one common point or axis in all of this. There is a consciousness that pervades everything, and the consciousness defines a boundary and assumes it to be an entity, and this becomes life.

Let us take a system – say the human body. It is comprised of an elaborate set of systems and processes, and feedback mechanisms, which by itself is great, but there needs to be an awareness that pervades this mechanism and assumes this system to be an entity – and thus a life is "born". As I said before, within the same physical system, nothing prevents consciousness from seeing a cell, or all cells or a group of cells, as a system. And thus many lives are possible in what we call the human body. For example, there is myself, Mohan, but there are many cells that are also alive. It is difficult to think of each organ also as a life, but conceptually, a heart or a lung also could be a living thing in the body. So between the cells as living things and Mohan as a living thing, there can also be heart, lung, skin, and other organs as living entities. As I mentioned before, the real and virtual alternate. Are the cells real or are the organs real? Are the organs real or is Mohan real?

Another example will show that life is indeed a continuum, and it is the identification of the consciousness with a system that we call life. Take a creeper plant like a betel leaf plant; it is one life as we all normally say. It creeps on the ground and sends roots continuously along its stem. Cut a piece of stem into two pieces, and you have two creepers. You could plant each one at a different house. Each creeper goes its own way and accumulates its own experiences. Similarly, to create a new variety of a rose, we could use a method called hybridization. The new plant gets the properties of both. Have we then, by our own action, created a life? It looks more like division. We would then say that, actually what is living is the cells and hence we have not created a life. Then can we say the plant is not living, or is it a virtual entity? The two creepers behave very differently and have different objectives from the cells that make them. I am not able to give an example in the animal kingdom because their existence relies on unique organs. For this reason, cutting one of them into two would not result in two lives. Neither is it possible to use the example of cutting off a hand off, because the separated hand is not a sustainable working model, whereas each piece of the creeper is. In the creeper, the same set of life-giving components is available at all places; hence, we can cut at random. In the case of a rose that is hybridized, is it not comparable to groups of people from different cultures being forced to come together to create a new culture? The question I am asking is, is the new plant a living entity, or are the cells from which it is hybridized living, or both? Years ago, people were sent from England to live in Australia. A smaller number of people from other countries also migrated to Australia. Can we then infer that a country is a living thing, and the people are also living?

From this example we see that life is continuous. It is actually the egos that are discrete. There was one ego (an attachment and an identification to a working system) associated to the whole creeper, and the ego divided in two when the creeper was divided into two new working systems. Hence there is something that is able to attach or identify itself to a working system, and assume that it is a life whereas it is purely arbitrary association.

So from these examples, we see that one of the conditions for a living being is to have a system over which something can assume control and call itself a living being. But this system definition and these boundaries are purely arbitrary, and there could be subsystems. Or this system could be part of a bigger system. It is actually possible to divide the same thing into multiple living beings, like the cells of a plant, the leaf, the plant itself. We can then extrapolate upwards and say that the forest is also living.

By this definition, are robots alive? From what we see in Isaac Asimov's novels or in Star Trek or the Terminator movies. After all, they have well-defined systems and feedback mechanisms, and they display an awareness of their surroundings. Are they then alive? I can only say that they are not alive in the same way as all the other living things we are familiar with like plants, animals are alive. The living things we are familiar with follow the Law of Correspondence. The living thing is made up of smaller living things, and the higher-order living thing is a virtual higher reality of the lower-level living entities (like the cells of the living thing). The robot, on the other hand, is made up of metal, which is not a living thing; hence, it does not follow the Law of Correspondence. It is just a thing created to mimic a living thing.

So the definition of life is that it should exhibit alternating virtual realities with an awareness of a system that it calls its own.

A robot does not exhibit this.

I am keenly aware that I have not said what it is that attaches itself to various systems, which enlivens the system. Conversely, if that thing withdraws itself, we say the system is dead. There is a whole lot of literature on "awareness", and many may even equate awareness to life. Awareness is definitely part of life, but awareness is not life. There needs to be an ego. Ego needs a sustainable system in which to store its experiences and hence call itself an independent living being. An important point to note is that this system is itself part of a higher system, and from that point of view, the lower one is nothing but part of itself. Now, where is this ego stored? Even a unicellular organism, which has life, has no place to store "awareness". In every living thing, the awareness "looks through" a particular physical system and gains impressions. As long as the awareness is looking through that physical system, we call the system alive. If the physical system is destroyed for any reason, the awareness withdraws itself. Then we say that the physical system is dead. We will see in later sections how awareness and energy are related, but awareness is like an instrument measuring a variable continuously. As an example, a thermometer measures the temperature at a particular point in time, but unless there is some mechanism for storing different readings, the concept of time will not be possible. Now if there is a mechanism that looks at the previous readings as well as the current readings, we see this record as "experience". The thing that is looking at these readings is the ego, the experiences are stored in a system, and awareness is that which faithfully reports a reading of a parameter. In our own lives, for example, we are made up of a collection of systems, which we call the body. Awareness is what enables us to collect observations, and since these are stored somewhere (in the brain?) we have a collection of experiences. Something is calling these experiences "my experiences", and this is the ego. So we need awareness, a system to store experiences, and something to make sense of these experiences. The third thing is the fundamental thing. We need to ask one more important question: Is this third thing same in all systems? Which means, there is only one thing across all living things and the variety we see is only different instruments and recordings. If we look at the dream state, definitely there is only one dreamer looking through all the characters in the dream. This should be true for our state as well by the Law of Correspondence.

Are Countries Living Things? What about Rivers and Mountains?

The funny thing is that a robot cannot be considered a living thing, but a legal entity like a company or a country may be considered living. This is because it is made up of lower-level living things that have identities and awareness of their own and owe allegiance to a common system. Other systems like rivers, mountains, seas, and the earth itself may also be living things. This is a possibility if consciousness enters them. The forest also exhibits the Law of Alternating Virtual Reality to be termed as a living being. However, like the cells in our bodies that have no clue as to how we feel or act, we cannot know how a mountain feels or reacts. A forest is made up of living things, and together, if the forest is a sustainable model, an ego could attach itself to it, making the forest a life form. This would satisfy the Law of Alternating Virtual Reality. The forest would then behave exactly as we would behave. Just as we harbour and encourage billions of bacteria in our bodies, which we consider beneficial, the forest also encourages visitors that can help its cause; say for example, butterflies and insects. If it does not like some animals that destroy its trees, it would develop thorns or poisons to ward off the animals. However, some systems are more stable and adaptable and hence we say that those life forms are real living beings whilst it is difficult to think of mountains and rivers as living things. However, please note if we do anything to make the forest happier, it would encourage us by giving what we want; in loose terms, if we pray to the forest god and treat it well, it will bless us.

Recently, one of the high courts of India passed a judgement that the rivers Ganga and Yamuna, the holiest rivers in India, are living entities and should be treated as such. It seems the Whanganui River in New Zealand has also been awarded such a status. There is a chapter in the constitution of Ecuador devoted to for the "rights of nature". Maybe these have been drafted to make administration of laws easier, but in my view, these natural wonders are really living entities as I have explained them.

Similarly, a country could be a living thing. Just as a living thing has a physical boundary and tries to accumulate energy and fight off other living things, a country either fights or cooperates with other living countries. A country requires the unflinching loyalty of its members and their dedication to do whatever is required for the country. Without this the country would die. It is not for the soldier to ask why he should lay down his life for a higher-level entity, but to just do his duty. Similarly, we would not like our white blood corpuscles to ask why they are required to fight infection rather than just live happily like the brain cells that do nothing but give instructions. A soldier cannot ask questions. Once he does, we can be sure that the country will die, just as we would die if the white blood corpuscles did not do their job. This is what patriotism is about.

So why is patriotism important? Without this fervour and unflinching loyalty, a country would collapse. It is also important for all citizens to exactly carry out their roles though they may be able to do better than other folks. To compare: if our kidney cells suddenly decided to roam around the body with the blood cells, we would instantly die! To an extent, young stem cells are free to roam around before taking up an assigned role, but once that is done, they cannot abandon roles. For example, if our white blood corpuscles decide not to fight, but rather to think strategy, we would die of the smallest infection. Similarly, our soldiers need to fight for our country, and any step by them not to fight would mean instant death for the country.

Our bodies are also designed to get a "kick" or a measure of pleasure when something we are associated with gets a boost. The experience we have when our favourite team wins is almost the same as the experience would be if we ourselves had achieved the win. We would feel the same sense of achievement. This principle is explained in more detail in the section called "Why Is Desire So Good?" Also, the pleasure we derive depends on the amount of the flow of energy, and this depends on the amount of buildup.

One thing to note here is that a fight at one level may look OK at another level. For example, if the earth is taken as a whole, a smaller country being eaten up by a larger one would be seen as mere consolidation; whereas for the smaller country it is war and death. When food is being eaten by a being, many others are dying. So it might be that, if we link ourselves to one level, we feel sorrow, while at a higher peace reigns.

How to Find Out If a System Is Living

It is time to define "life".

Most of us assume we know what is living. We think of plants and animals. The reverse question is this: Can things that we normally don't think as living be considered living? This is an important question. To give examples: a company, a forest, a river, a thought, one's dream world. Are these living? Why not a robot? How do we define life precisely so that entities can either be excluded or included?

All life forms are made up of systems that consist of members. The members themselves are systems, and themselves have sub members. For a system to be sustainable, every member should play a role that helps each other member. Taken together, these members keep the living thing in harmony with its environment. The system should be so designed that every member is loyal to the group or is forced to comply. Any living system lives in an environment, which itself is a system. The environment, along with other members like itself, forms a higher system. In and through all this is "something" that attaches itself to the systems. This "thing" itself is an entity. On each system it attaches itself to, experiences are recorded. These collections of experiences give rise to an "ego". The ego is what we see as a living thing. When the loyalty of the members changes, or the environment changes, the system becomes unstable, and the "thing" withdraws itself. We call this death.

You can see that I am struggling for words as I write this definition. I have resisted using typical jargon like "God".

You can see the Law of Alternating Virtual Reality in operation in this definition. Let me give an example. I will analyze this later in depth, but let us analyze our thoughts when we are dreaming. In my dream state, I have thoughts. They operate in an environment, which is nothing but our dream world. Now, my dream world itself is a system with its own thoughts; in fact, there are numerous thoughts all interacting with each other. Each one of them is living, but in and through all of them, there is an "I" which enlivens them. This is the "thing" I was talking about in the above definition. The "I" in the dream may or may not take part in the interactions, but definitely, without the "I", there is no dream or thoughts within it. None of the members below seem to recognize this fact. They behave as if they were themselves living things independently (which they are in a sense). All thoughts in the dream, all characters, have accumulated experiences, which make them assume that they are individuals in their own right. Now, a thought itself is made up of multiple entities; for example, a thought is made up of emotions, feelings, and memories. Two thoughts can join together and create a new thought. This new thought again has a seemingly independent existence. That which makes up a thought need not be another thought. For example, each entity that makes up a Mohan need not look like me. Each thought has an ego; in that sense, it has an identity.

The most important thing in this example is that it is the "I" that enlivens the thoughts. Without the attention of the "I" in the dream, a thought will perish. Thus the attention of the "I" is the energy for thoughts. In a similar way, is the attention of what we call God, our energy? Is energy God? We will discuss the important point about energy later. To keep the system in order, energy is required. Attention of the higher level results in higher energy. Without energy, the systems stop, resulting in death, but energy itself is not life.

The concept of "I" is further discussed in the section "Commonality of all levels".

Now let us apply this definition to some life forms. We will deal with the obvious ones first: Is an animal a living thing? It has a set of systems (organs, which carry out necessary processes) which themselves are made up of cells, and the cells themselves are systems. All organs and cells obey a set of rules and are in turn benefitted. Each animal has a place to store its experiences, and therefore has an ego, "I". Therefore it exhibits alternate virtual reality, has an awareness of its experience, and is hence living.

The Law As It Is Applied to the Physical Plane

The best example we can see is that of the microscopic atom and its electrons. This structure seems to be similar to the sun and the planets, which again seem to be similar to stars and galaxies. A hard, physical object like, say, a rock, is nothing inside but vast empty spaces with planet-like objects whirling around. A rock next to another rock is like one galaxy next to another one. Of course we can project it to the extent we know upwards or downwards, but the pattern is repeating. Thus what is "inside" is similar to what is "outside".

There is evidence that matter is also another lower order form of energy ($E=mc^2$). If this is so, the Law of Correspondence will be a given, as everything inside or outside will be the same thing.

The Law As Applied to the Mental Plane

There is a correspondence between the "real" world and our mental world. Our creation is all of the thoughts we have created and have enjoyed. When our minds are full of thoughts, we do some housekeeping and encourage only the thoughts we want to remain. However as we all know we are only sometimes successful. Creating thoughts is easy; making them useful to us and managing each thought along with the others to give us the environment and experience we want is very difficult. Additionally, it is almost impossible to "kill" a thought.

We can correspond thoughts with the real world because both are living things. Living things need energy, and they eat other living things or get energy from the sun. Thoughts, too, act like living things. They have individuality, a life, and a life span. Thoughts, too, need energy, and they acquire energy either from other thoughts or from our attention. Hence our attention is the equivalent of the energy from the sun. Light energy in the real world corresponds to awareness in the mental plane.

Our thoughts exist in our mental plane and are created and nurtured to coexist with the other thoughts we have already created. For the most part, thoughts are offshoots of other thoughts and are similar to living things and are bred of other living things. Thoughts spawn off other child thoughts. They require energy to survive, and their main source of energy is our attention. A poor alternative could be that they get energy by feeding off other fellow thoughts, not unlike what goes on in our world.

Let us try to draw the comparison between our "real world" and our mental word. In our real world, different species of living things dwell. In our mental world, different species of thoughts dwell. Thoughts are our internal world, and the world outside should mirror the internal world according to the Law of Correspondence. The point to note is that, in the real world, there is now new material needed if we consider the entire ecosystem of the earth. All things need energy, which comes from the sun. The plants are the only entities that trap the energy from sunlight, and everything else feeds off that. Similarly, *sattvic* thoughts (pure, calm and thoughts which want to do good to others) get most of their energy from the "sun" of our minds, which is awareness. They are like plants; they just absorb awareness for their supply of energy. (*Sattvic* food in this context refers to food that is nourishing and soothing.) There are thoughts like jealousy and anger that feed on other thoughts and are like carnivorous beings. They feed on sattvic thoughts.

In the real world, we eat and digest energy-giving food, spend the energy through exercise, and excrete the part from which we cannot extract any more energy. These are the three basic actions – eat, exercise, and excrete.

We can see the parallel in the laws of thermodynamics as well. Any engine that converts energy into another form of energy cannot fully convert the input energy. In fact, the most theoretically efficient engine is the Carnot engine. It takes in energy from a higher temperature source and puts out energy to a lower energy source. The efficiency is given by the formula $1-T_2/T_1$ where T_1 is the higher temperature and T_2 is the lower temperature. It is also equal to $1-Q_2/Q_1$ where Q_2 is the energy rejected and Q_1 is the energy taken in. It further goes to say that Q_2 can never be zero, or in other words, some egestion (excretion in other contexts) has to happen.

As in the external world, in the mental world too we take in energy and have to excrete some energy.

In the mental world, we eat thoughts, exercise or work out our thoughts, and excrete thoughts, so we have to be very careful in defining what activities define these three in the mental world.

In the mental world, the thoughts we entertain in the beginning of the cycle are filled with energy; in other words, eating. This happens, for example, when we fantasize, daydream, wish that something were true, or imagine how good we would feel if a particular thing were to happen.

We then analyze, decide, rationalize, and communicate, which are all mental exercises like physical exercises.

Then, lastly, the very same thoughts that we "ate" are slowly excreted. This is a very important step, one which very few can do right. It is very important to excrete in the physical world; otherwise, we cannot eat anything new. Whatever is inside would burst through and come out at one time or another. Now, in our world we control this phenomenon very well. We have bathrooms built for this purpose, and we try to have fixed timings for elimination. Imagine what would happen in the real world if we excreted wherever and whenever we wanted to, or strictly stopped this activity, as it is unpleasant. Waste product would just burst out in the middle of your analysis or while you were eating.

Since all the three activities deal with thoughts, there could be some unpleasant things. Imagine if, in the real world, you tried to eat what you have excreted. It would be so distasteful we cannot even think about it. But that is exactly what most of us do in the mental world. When you are sitting quietly in the morning, you are thinking some thoughts. The question to ask yourself is, am I in the process of eating, exercising, or excreting my thoughts? Let us say there is a thought that you took in yesterday. It was tasty when you ate the thought, and it has run its course of energy. The undigested thought is now on its way out. You now remember how great it felt yesterday, and you try to "eat" that same thought again. Now your attention to the thought is energy, and the same thought gets a new lease on life and gets back into the food cycle. The right thing to do, of course, would be to let it pass. Just keep observing the thought on its way out, without entertaining it in any way. Otherwise, what would happen? You would be eating your own excreta

28

and would be unable to take in anything new. Suppose you decide that the all of this is most distasteful, and you decide also to stop excreting altogether. Whatever is inside would burst out when you are eating something else or when you are analyzing.

We set aside a place and time for bathroom activities. Do we set time to eject thoughts after they are digested? If we don't, when we least expect them, we may experience nasty consequences.

Here is another interesting observation. You watch an exciting movie. The first time you see it, you are full of attention and enjoy yourself immensely. You derive a lot of energy from this experience. This is the greatest movie of all time. However, you cannot see it more than twice or thrice. If you are dull witted, or the subject matter is heavy, perhaps you can see it a few more times. Why does an experience that gives us great joy the first time not give us the same joy later? Actually this is the reason that the movie industry is active, and also due to the same reason, why the world is running. We derive energy from the thought, and after we have extracted all that we can from it, a second round of the same thing is like trying to eat our own digested food again. At the most, we can digest what we could not in the first round. That is why we need the movie industry to churn out one movie after another, one album after another, and, in fact, the world to produce new experiences again and again. The brain lights up only when it sees something new.

Another interesting phenomenon is why we argue too much. All of us need energy just as all our thoughts need energy. The "thought energy" we are talking about is not food; rather, it is attention from the higher level. But not many of us know how to connect to this higher level for energy. So we try to grab it from others. We demand attention from others. We engage them in some way on any point and then get into an argument. The basic mechanism of an argument is that we convince someone of a point, and if the other agrees, we win the energy we put forward. If the other person does not agree, he or she puts forward an argument and some energy. Now the energy at stake is, first, the energy we put in. Then the energy put in by the other person is added. If we put in more energy and convince the other, then we gain all this energy. So we put in more energy to gain the energy put forth by both. Slowly the stakes become higher until what is at stake is a huge pile of energy. This is similar to a popular card game. One player plays a card, and then the second player plays a card. If the cards match, the pile below is the second players pile. If not the first player plays again and checks if he has a match. Else the pile below keeps getting bigger. The pile at stake is getting larger. We have to win this at any cost. So our arguments become more and more silly. Any third person who just comes in might wonder why people are arguing such a silly point. Eventually one person loses the argument, thereby losing all the energy. That is why we feel so down after losing an argument. We also feel anger at that person for having stolen our energy. What is the way out? Not putting forward the energy is one way, meaning that we do not engage in an argument. But other people often force us into arguments. Or, maybe we ourselves feel confident that we can win the energy from the other person by putting in the bare minimum of energy and then getting away. There is also one other way. After we lose the argument, we can connect to the higher source for energy so we don't have to depend on energy from others.

This also manifests in personality types. Some people are content with their own energy; they don't need additional energy from others. They are happy regardless of their external surroundings. They derive energy from some other source, not from other people or pets. Some hunt for energy from their friends, parents, teachers, or sometimes even their own kids. This manifests as finding fault, arguing, scolding, and so forth. The other set of people strategies to prevent others from taking the energy. For example, they answer in monosyllables only. This is a closed personality whose strategy is to lose the least amount of energy, if any at all. The other person is trying to hook him, either by taunts or by challenges. These attackers and closed personalities occur in all families. In fact, the roles can oscillate. If the parent is a closed personality, the kids pester him or her for attention. These kids, when they grow up, pester their own kids. Now their kids become the close type of personality, and the cycle continues.

Then there is a wide range of eating disorders. Supposing you have eaten too many thoughts. Digestion may suffer, and diseases like diabetes may set in. If we take in too many "spicy" thoughts (salacious material, gossip, or jealous thoughts), we will get too much acidity and heartburn. My theory, which everyone must prove for himself or herself, is that there is a connection between the thoughts and the physical body. When the mind and body are calm, an introduction of a spicy thought produces a sort of burning within the body. It is quite difficult to explain, but we feel a heat or a burning inside. If we continue too much of the same thing, we lose sensitivity and take that as "normal". Similarly, too many thoughts could produce diseases related to overeating like diabetes and obesity. People following the Transcendental Meditation techniques have done some experiments about correlations between lowering our thoughts and improving overall health.

Every living being (including every thought in the mental world) wants energy. How do we get more energy in the mental world? In the physical world, as I mentioned, by thinking that we are pushing the car, but not actually doing so, we can get energy flowing into our body. The mind is the valve that controls how much energy we generate. Similarly, try this experiment: Think a thought that excites you and normally gives you a great deal of pleasure. This usually is a thought that requires or generates high energy, which is why it gives pleasure. Now suddenly stop thinking about that thought and leave the mind blank. The energy flow continues for some time, and since we are not thinking that thought, energy is not spent either. This exercise increases the energy in our mental plane. As our mind is the valve that allows energy to flow into the physical body, the "will" or the intellect is what regulates the flow into the mental plane.

Most of these ideas are already echoed in our scriptures and symbolism. *Brahma* (the creator), *Vishnu* (maintainer), and *Shiva* (the destroyer) are one, and that one entity assumes separate forms depending on whether he is creating, maintaining, or destroying living things. Similarly, in our mental plane we do the same. Just by our imaginations we create a thought or a species of thought. Similarly, God can create anything in this plane by a mere wish. As God is above us, we are above our thoughts. Each of our thoughts, in its own right, is a living entity. Each of us is God, for our thought world.

Even among Hindu gods, there is a god and also a god above the god. Hence we have Rudra (an aspect of Shiva) and above him *Shiva*, *Vishnu* and *Maha Vishnu*, *Siva* and *Parama Siva*, and so forth. This is another example for alternating virtual reality.

Understanding the Mind by Understanding the World

In any field, control of the mind is very important. In fact it is the only differentiator in the determination of a winner, and ultimately it is the person who has control over his or her mind who wins. In the kung fu movies, the guru is always someone who has control over his own mind. So it is in sports, in the arts, in stock market investing, as well as academic studies – in any aspect of life.

If it is so vital, it is imperative to understand the mind before we can control it. Of course this is a subject on which all spiritual leaders have elaborated. In fact, this seems to be the basic first step as well as the last step. Once you control your mind, it is said, the wall between you and God breaks down. Mind can be defined as the flow of thoughts.

How does one control the mind? If the mind is the flow of thoughts, then we need to control the thoughts in number, in speed, and in quality. The mind is like a giant river that is roaring with huge volume, velocity and muddiness. Any feeble attempt to control it is useless, and strong efforts on our side will wash us away. The mighty river is nothing but a huge collection of harmless drops. Similarly the mind is nothing but the collection of a large number of thoughts.

The thing to note is that every thought behaves exactly like a living thing. Once it is born, it will strive to continue living. It will make friends; it will get energy either from your attention or from other thoughts by killing them. It will associate with other thoughts to form a mass that has a better chance to hook our attention.

What rules do we need to apply to control our thoughts? Let us apply the Law of Correspondence in the reverse; that is, let us understand our minds, see what is happening in what we call the real world, and apply it to our minds. Let us consider an ideal society (if you can find one).

We see the following are required for a good society:

1) All members of society are governed by strong rules, which everyone agrees to. If they do not agree, they are sent out or prevented from mixing in society until they are reformed. All members follow the rules, sometimes suppressing their desires, for the sake of the overall good. Not all members understand this, and left to themselves will breach the rules. A strong punishment mechanism must be in place for those who do this.

2) All members have defined roles. The roles so defined are mutually helpful to each other, while allowing each person to express his or her individuality. The individual should perform his or her role, to its fullest, before pursuing other desires. The ideal would be to match the desire and role.

3) Every member must be free to express himself or herself, without forcing others to follow. Killing one another, unless as defined by the rules, is strictly prohibited.

4) A sustainable model must be made. The members should be a good mix of the old and young, the wise and the learners, the doers and the thinkers, and all of them must be enjoying themselves.

Here are some observations about society that have parallels in the thought world:

1) The union of two beings produces a third. It is very rare for a being to be born from a single being. It is not known how the first being was born. Generally, a being needs nourishment and protection when just born. Generally speaking, birds of a feather flock together.

2) There are multiple circumstances that control the population in society:

a) A change of environment, which breaks down the structure; for example, fire, drowning, crushing, poisoning, etc.

b) A lack of input energy; for example, starving of air or food.

c) Disease, which introduces a second species to eliminate the first

d) Prevention of new births

3) It is very difficult to kill a single being without collateral damage.

4) It is normal for one species to eat another species. In fact, all the animal kingdom derives its food from plants or other animal beings.

5) The universal source of energy for us is the sun. The equivalent in the mind space is our attention.

A healthy mind has a good mix of thoughts – some old, some new. All get adequate exposure to our attention. Some are less evolved thoughts and get less of our attention and are eaten by other thoughts. In other words, they get displaced, and the new thought gets our attention.

Assume that you have an exam and want to study. You sit down and try to create some blank space in your mind and pay attention to the thoughts regarding what you are reading. These thoughts get your attention and thereby your energy. But the other thoughts in your mind are not fools. With the energy they already possess, they displace the study thoughts. Now, it is not chronological order that determines which thoughts remain uppermost in your mind; rather, it is the amount energy possessed by the thoughts. So, normally, the thoughts that have the most intensity come to your attention. We refer to this as the mind becoming distracted. The more the energy contained in the side thoughts, the more difficult it is to concentrate on what you want to focus on (your studies). You proceed with more determination now. You give more attention to the study subjects. It may work if you can create greater energy for them; otherwise, you will become distracted again. This has serious consequences. Imagine a sportsman is facing a ball and, at the moment the ball is approaching him, his mind starts thinking about a fight he had the day before. You can imagine the result.

One way out of this is to reduce the side thoughts. However, the number of thoughts we have created is too huge for this. At the most we can create a small window of time – a second maybe for most, and a minute for more adept people – in which we can devote our undivided attention. Then the side thoughts take over once more. The irony is that we ourselves have given energy to those thoughts at one time and are now helpless to control them.

We could try other tricks as well. Suppose we announce that we are doing a *satsang*, or meeting, with like-minded people and we will gather to talk only about spiritual topics and positive ideas for self-improvement. Or we could say that we will talk only about the good qualities of other people. We could do it for an hour or so. After that we cannot hold onto the same thoughts. There are only so many "good thoughts" you can think about! So if you decide to sit for an hour and think only good-quality thoughts, the number of thoughts is reduced. It is the same in our mental plane. If we change the direction of thoughts towards worthy goals, or towards how to help others, we quickly run out of ideas and, therefore, reduce the number of thoughts.

Another idea would be to starve our thoughts. We starve them by not giving them our attention. If the thought comes to our attention, we don't engage it in any way. It comes, it dances, and when we don't bother about it, it sheepishly goes away, hoping to catch your attention another time. But starving one particular thought is very difficult. If you want to, you can starve all thoughts, but that would create a huge revolt if the number of thoughts is large! So meditation to still your thoughts cannot be done in the initial stages. Better to try to do *japa* (direction of thoughts) or social work (quality of thoughts) first.

In summary, the way to control thoughts is to either reduce the quantity of thoughts, change the direction of thoughts, or change the quality of thoughts. In fact, all three are inter-related, and we need to attempt to improve all aspects. The irony is that we built the energy ourselves, as if we were turning a giant flywheel and making it spin faster and faster. Now we cannot stop it. If we try to hold it still, either we are thrown away, or we break the flywheel. The only safe way is to stop giving it more energy and hope it stops on its own slowly. Or we could apply opposite forces in a controlled way.

Why do we need to control our thoughts? For joy and ecstasy. I will explain this in the section called, "Energy Flow Is the Most Enjoyable Thing".

The Commonality in All Levels

The commonality in all living things is that there is an observer "I". Truly speaking, we are only sure that the "I" in the real world is only an observer and all the other living things we see may or may not be living; they may be just our imaginations. This is similar to our mental world and our dream world. There is the "I" who is observing all the thoughts and dreams, and all other thoughts seem to have a life of their own and are trying to coexist. This can be compared to a "species" of living things found in the external world: "species" of thoughts might be anger, jealousy, love, compassion, and so forth.

With some thinking, we can see that the "I" in the real world is the same "I" in the mental and dream world. This definition of "I" is derived from the realm of spirituality. However from this explanation it can be seen that, if it is the same "I" in everything, the fundamental nature of everything should be the same. This is another corollary of the Law of Correspondence and a great statement of spirituality. You are God. *Tat Twam Asi* is a *mahavakya* (a great statement) in spirituality that means "Thou art that". From this explanation, for the cells in the levels below you, you are god. But since you are the same being at all levels below you and this principle applies to one level above you, you are yourself god at this level. This is because it is the same "I" at levels below and above you. In mathematics, there is a logic, if it is true for any number "n" and it is true for the number 1, and if it is true for the number "n+1" it is true for all numbers. The fundamental point is the "I" in all these levels. That is the basis of the Law of Correspondence. If the "I" is same in all levels, does it not stand to reason that all levels are fundamentally the same?

If we assume that the world below (our mental plane) is created by us, there is someone who must have created what we call the real world. Whenever we create a thought, we do so by filling it with some energy. The energy given will take it to some extent and time. The life of a thought can be compared to the life of a person. The intention is that this thought will branch out and display all its facets for our enjoyment, but there are already a host of thoughts vying for our attention, and they may or may not allow this new thought to be nurtured to maturity.

Now to do an experiment: If we make a conscious decision not to entertain a thought in any way (which itself is tricky because the act of trying to ignore a thought actually is attention to the thought!), we see that that particular thought dies. Normally it is not difficult for a thought to die because there are other thoughts competing for our attention, each thought requiring energy to keep itself alive. Thus the energy of our thought world is our attention – awareness or consciousness of the thought. Applied above, our own energy is the attention our creator gives to us.

Hence "awareness" or "consciousness" is the common axis, theme, or basis on which the entire world exists. This somehow brings in the "energy" we need to do things. This is what all living things in all worlds are after – attention from the being above. Later we see that it is the flow of energy is the one which gives us joy and this is exactly what all living things are after.

Correspondence Between Dreams and Our Real World

In our mental plane and in our dreams, as in our "real world", there is an individual "I", who is an observer who creates, maintains, and destroys thoughts and ideas. In the dream state, we start by creating a thought that interacts with the other thoughts already in place, and very soon we have a complex world similar to the waking world. We create and maintain thoughts and then destroy them to make way for other thoughts just as our creator is doing in our "real" world. The correspondence between the real world and the dream world is well documented in many religions. There is this story about a king who dreamt he was a butterfly. He woke up and asked everybody whether he was a king dreaming he was a butterfly or a butterfly dreaming he was a king. The answer given him by his guru was that both are dreams. Suppose a boy is dreaming he is a king. To the dream King, the boy is the god as the boy is at a higher level and can pretty much change the story of the king as the boy wishes. However, the King himself may dream that he is a beggar. To the dream beggar, the king is the god.

In the waking world, we have many experiences, and our bodies and minds need rest. The mind needs to work out a particular problem and try out various alternatives and see which ones succeed. The failed ones are discarded. A species of thoughts is created and taken to a logical conclusion. The train of thought in the dream is energized if it is found to be attractive or able to solve a problem, but it can be wiped out in a jiffy and replaced by another set of thoughts. Is this not similar to how a species is suddenly created, and then, after a while, disappears? Why do many species show evolution, slowly, as though there was some mass experiment going on as improvements develop slowly? If God was all knowing, why did he not use the best design in the beginning? Well, why did our best idea not come to us in the beginning? In my reasoning, we should not be too much worried about so many species going extinct. The dreamer above us wants it that way. He can recreate in a flash, and also erase us in a flash, just as we would do to our dream characters.

In our dream state, we observe many events and experience many feelings. We are faced with problems, difficulties, and challenges much as we are in the waking world. On closer analysis, there are actually two "I" personalities in the dream. One is the "I" that is involved in the dream world and faces all the troubles. Another "I" is the one that is observing all these things and suddenly realizes that this is a dream and remembers both the dream and the waking state (for a brief moment at least). Notice that this "I" was very closely aligned with the dream state to the extent that the difference was not noticed and was common to both the states. Once awake, the first "I", which I call the lower-level "I", ceases to exist, and the higher-level "I" takes over. (to make matters more confusing, there is an observer "I" observing both the dream and waking states!).

Another point to notice is that the higher-level "I" is the one that wanted to enter the dream state. It made preparations to fall asleep. The purpose of falling asleep was to clear up some mental clutter, go over the day's events, work out a few possibilities for solving the vexing issues of the day, or just think of some pleasant thoughts and anticipate some pleasant things. Thus the higher-level "I" had an agenda when it went into the dream state. It wanted to enter the dream state for its own entertainment. Another important point is that the higher level "I" had a plan as to when he wanted to wake up.

Observing deeper, we see that, in the initial stages of sleep, the higher-level "I" is very much an active part and does some amount of "directing" as to what thoughts are to be dreamt about. It even sometimes jumps into the dream and changes the course of the dream events. Slowly, the higher-level "I" loses control, and the dream characters, including the lower-level "I", behave in a similar constrained way in the dream. Please note that falling asleep is gradual, and the awareness of being in a dream state slowly envelops the dreamer. But the waking up is sudden, and the overlap is generally shorter during the wake-up stage. The waking up is either due to a cessation of the agenda if the higher-level "I", an elapsed time, an external event like an alarm, or a nightmare.

Our earth period is also divided into four periods. The first period is a golden period, and subsequent periods slowly become more and more decadent.

It is said in the scriptures that a *yuga* is an epoch or era within a four-part cycle. The first yuga is a golden period in which everyone is, in general, virtuous, and gods come in and intervene at the required times and are generally more accessible. In the second yuga, it requires a god to be born in our midst and be a shining example to all living things. The problems faced and the ethical dilemmas presented are not so complicated. Rules are laid and followed. In the next yuga, the ethical dilemmas are more complex. People follow the law but not the spirit of the law. It requires god to intervene and point out the spirit of the law in a detailed way. The current Yuga is supposed to be the *Kali Yuga*, where the gods are not accessible. Law and order becomes more and more complicated and difficult. Finally in the end, in an abrupt way, the *kali yuga*, the last and darkest yuga, ends, and there is a sudden awakening! Compare this with our process of falling asleep, the involvement of the higher-level "I", and its involvement in the dreams, and later getting into a deep sleep state where the higher-level "I" is not available, and suddenly it is awakened. Are they not remarkably similar?

As in the lower (dream) level so it is in the higher.

What does this mean for us? You are living in the dream of a higher entity. You may want to invoke and call god. Do you wake up to solve the problems you are currently facing? We either play by the rules currently on, or we wake up and rewrite the rules. The problem with waking up is that everything we were currently "enjoying" becomes totally irrelevant.

There are various phases of sleep. During the first one, we are generally aware of the thoughts we are thinking. Most probably they reflect what we did during the day or the hopes and fears of tomorrow.

However, the thoughts here don't run away unchecked. The thoughts have a certain logic to them, each with a link to the previous one. Then we let go of the control. This is necessary if we are to sleep. However, once we let go of the control, for some time the thoughts continue along the same line of logic. But then they start to deteriorate in logic and linkages. In general, might is right here: the strongest thoughts – fear, for example – dominate, but still there is a carry forward of the previous stage of control, so it is quickly brought under control. Otherwise, we would regain full control, or in other words, wake up. With the third phase we experience further deterioration, and thoughts are very difficult to control. In the fourth stage, all semblance of law and order is lost, and thoughts become weak as well. There is no rationale connected to the thoughts, and it is in this stage that our deepest fears surface – tigers chase us, teachers scold us, colleagues laugh at us, and we are not in control. Again it is possible to have pleasant thoughts of winning the match or getting a lot of money may also come. And then we suddenly wake up; for example, when the alarm goes off. In an instant, the entire dream world is gone. There is a brief moment during which we consider going back to the dream world so we can try to teach that tiger a lesson. That is why alarms have snooze buttons. Since control is restored in the mental world, again there is sanity, law, and order in the mental world.

Correspondence Between Diseases and the Mental Plane

This is also well documented, and now common knowledge. There is even a set of psychosomatic diseases that is universally recognized. The Law of Correspondence states that the state of the internal is reflected externally. Basically, our mental harmony is reflected into the outer world. If there is a set of thoughts rebelling against the general body of thoughts, this can prevent the achievement of harmony. At the cellular level, this can manifest as cancer. Similarly, by the Law of Correspondence, I can postulate, to be verified of course, that an excess of thought creation is similar to an excess in food intake. In short, more "thought food" will create conditions in the mind similar to the conditions in the body caused by excess food intake. We will later see how we excrete our undigested food, we need to excrete our leftover thoughts.

Acupuncture is based on the fact that some parts of the external body correspond to the organs inside. In the book the holographic evidence, it was said that the Chinese discovered the man in the ear. The ear looks like a foetus, and stimulating that region somehow affects the organ we want to rectify. This is another example of as it is inside so it is outside.

I read somewhere that cancer cells are always present in the body. It is just that, when they are not detectable in numbers, we say that we are fine. Cancer is actually a set of cells that does not owe allegiance to any of the systems in our body; they want to go their own way. They are not interested in doing their duty and feel that their interests are better served by moving away from the group. This is similar to a bunch of people in a country who want to start a separate country. (We have mentioned that a country can be considered be a living thing.) A country exists successfully just because all citizens are loyal to the country. If sufficient numbers of citizens break away, the country collapses. It is another matter whether the new country survives or not. Similarly, a group of thoughts could encourage revolt or alienation from the current system; this is similar to the actions of cancerous cells. This could happen if one set of thoughts hates the other thoughts; for example, one part of us might hate what we did the other day, or one set of thoughts might make us behave in an objectionable way. Such a situation, according to the Law of Correspondence, should trigger a matching response in the body as well. There is also a theory that a specific set of thoughts can trigger changes in the body. There is the legend that a king who was in good shape, within a matter of hours after hearing devastating news, showed signs of aging, including white hair. This is also available for our own observation. When we have worrisome thoughts, we easily catch cold. When we are happy, we are able to maintain good health. Jealous thoughts and thoughts of anger have deep impact on the corresponding parts of the heart, stomach, and other parts of the body.

Thus there is more to the statement: "You are what you think".

The Law as It Is Applied to the Spiritual Plane

Before I begin, I need to briefly define what I mean by spiritual. We have seen that there are levels below us, like the organs, cells, and so on. The levels above us I term as spiritual. This is, of course, purely relative because when we move up one level, there are more spiritual levels above.

Our Relationship to God

With all this theory, could we apply the Law of Correspondence to God and our relationship with God? From the phenomenon of alternating virtual reality, we are the god to the levels below us, and for all of us there is a god above us. As I mentioned before, I am completely dependent on the loyalty of the organs and cells below me to be loyal to the concept of Mohan as a god; otherwise, the system would break down and the structure called Mohan would not exist. The organs and cells below me, on the one hand, can never see me or know me. Also, it does not matter if they believe in me or not, as long as they do their job. I, on the other hand, will try to keep all of the organs and cells happy and provide them with what they need. This has been what we have seen before.

Now we also take the parallel between the dream state and the waking state. We have seen that the "I" in the waking state and the

"I" in the dream state are the same, and from the point of the dreamer "I", the waking "I" is god. As soon as I wake up, if I decide to go back to my dream world, I can go back and re-write the dream the way I want. In short, I am the god of my dream world. Another important point is that in and through all the characters of the dream, as well as nonliving things in the dream, I am present. In fact, all that is there in the dream is nothing but me. With this background, let us look at some the statements made about God.

God is present everywhere. This corresponds to me being present everywhere in my dream.

God is all powerful. This corresponds to me being able to do anything I want in my dream.

God created us. This corresponds to me creating my dream for my own entertainment.

God is in all forms but no form defines god. This corresponds to the forms I have as my body and organs, but I am more than any particular organ of the body. Also in the dream world I am all forms, living and non living, but I am not anyone in the dream.

Similarly you can extrapolate that God is an omniscient, omnipotent, all pervading creator and destroyer. And you can continue to extrapolate any other statement made about God. You could also justify statements that are contradictory: God has no form; he is in all forms. Just like Mohan is not formed like any of the organs, but still contains all the forms of the organs. God is formless, as Mohan is just a concept as far as the cells are concerned.

What Is Death? What Happens When We Die?

Perhaps these are the most challenging questions we ask. We can understand death a little better by applying the Law of Correspondence. Consider that you are the god of your mental world. What happens when a thought dies? The question is rather funny because, as far as you are concerned, nothing happens. This is because we consider a thought alive when it receives some energy. When the energy is finished, the thought has no action and you are completely unaware of it. However, in some seed form it is tucked away somewhere, and just when you remember it, it again springs back to life. However, this time the environment of the other thoughts may be different. This is similar to the different birth and rebirth cycle of the Hindus. So to question what happens when a thought dies does not make sense to us. Basically it was a bundle of energy, a virtual thing, and it came from me and just merged into me. Similarly, asking God what happens when we die would not make sense to him because you, yourself, are virtual. Only he exists, so there is no point splitting hairs on a virtual topic.

However, some questions remain. We see the dead person's body. Why don't we see the dead thought's body? The answer is from the perspective. From the perspective of a living thing at the same level as the thought, the living thing might be able to see it. But from the perspective of a god in his higher level (in this case yourself), the god cannot. That is because the moment you remember the thought, it once again becomes alive. From your god-like perspective nothing is alive or dead; it is just that some thoughts have energy and thereby some activities while others are away from your consciousness and are therefore without energy. Death does not make sense in the way we define it in real life.

To understand this, we can look at the parallel in the mental plane and the parallel between dreaming and waking up.

We are the creators of our thoughts. We see that each thought is a bundle of energy that is born, fights for energy, and dies when it gets no attention from the higher source. The question is, what happens to the bundle of energy when it gets out of the thought structure? From our standpoint, the thought that used to occupy our mental space is gone. However, the energy associated with it is absorbed by other living thoughts. This is similar to what happens in our physical world. When a person dies, the body is food for other living organisms. The thought as a living thing was actually a bundle of our own consciousness looking through a structured material. From our viewpoint, the thought had no business to assume it was anything more than that. If it had any individuality or an ego, it was purely *maya* (illusion) because the only thing that existed was ourselves permeating all our thoughts. Thus, from our viewpoint, there was a bundle of energy that gave us feedback and entertained us for some time. Thereafter, following a breakdown of structure, it went back to our consciousness. We don't understand what is meant by the death of a thought as a life form; much less are we worried about it because we can always recreate it. So from a higher viewpoint, death is no big deal. In fact, if thoughts didn't die after they have entertained us, we would have a big problem.

However, there could be something that moves from one thought to another thought. A thought has many properties; for example, it has energy, it has details, it has an emotion, and it has linkages to other thoughts. This is a structure, and like our physical structure, it exists to keep it stable. The more emotion, the more linkages, the stronger the thought is. However, on its death (the breakdown of the structure), the emotion attached to it is still around. This is similar to the way a general sadness remains even after we stop thinking our particular sad thoughts. A new thought arises, and it picks up new details and new linkages, but the underlying emotion is the same. A happy thought ends but all other thoughts seem better due to the positive energy of the previous thought. That is why we say, one good word could make our day. A new thought born in this atmosphere is a rebirth of the previous thought. The old structure is gone, but it retains some aspect of the old thought. In that sense, it is a rebirth. Now, the new thought will behave and have experiences dictated by what it carries from the previous emotions, which we can say in a way is the fate of the new thought. Thus the emotion of a thought at the time of death is of utmost importance to the thought that will take its place.

Krishna, in the Bhagavad Gita, says that the mental and emotional makeup of a person at the time of death is the only thing that matters. It does not matter if the person lived a sinful life; if at the time of death the person is pious, he or she will get a great rebirth. There are many stories on this topic including the one about lighting the lamp in the holy month. In this story, a pious priest in a temple used to do great service in the temple. One day, his wife, who was having an affair with another person, came to the temple. It was dark, and she tore a bit of fabric from her sari to use in the lamp so she could see her lover. The priest saw this, and it enraged him. In a brief scuffle, he pushed his wife, and she was pierced by the *trishul* (trident) in the temple. Upon death, the husband went to the worst hell because he killed someone in the temple, whilst the wife went to the highest heaven because she lit a lamp during the holy month even though unwittingly. While on the face of it, the outcome looks unfair, we have learned why it is that way.

Our Own Death Is Not Possible

While it is easy to understand the death of others as a loss of energy, what about our own death? Well, by applying the Law of Correspondence between the dream world and the real world, we can see that our own death is not possible. (Caution: in the dream state there is an "I" in the dream and there is an "I" watching the dream. We are talking about the second one. It is entirely possible that the first "I" dies and the second one watches it.)

In the dream world, there is an "I". This corresponds to the "I" in our waking state. In the dream state I go from one dream to another. In the waking state I go from one experience to another or from one circumstance to another or, for those who believe in rebirth, from one birth to another. In both states, the "I" continues. In the dream state, all dreams are finished when I wake up, and to the extent of the dream world, I, the dreamer is dead. But from the point of view of the waking "I", the right thing to say would be that the dream world is dead and gone. Similarly, if we apply the law, the "I" in the waking state cannot die; it just wakes up in another role or wakes from the entire dream. In other words, this entire world, as we see it now, ends, and I wake up to another world. Shall we then say that this world as we see it is unreal, yet similar to the dream world? Yes. In fact, that is the basis of one of the Upanishads (ancient Sanskrit Hindu texts) called the Mandukya Upanishad. It says that both the dream world and the waking world are maya, or an illusion, and the waking world looks real because we have more instruments with which to observe it (all the sense organs of the body), whereas in the dream world we have only the mind. It is possible to come out of both these dreams and realize another "I" which has awakened from both these dreams. In this sense, the "I" never dies; in fact, the worlds die! What a conclusion!

This also seems to send some logical basis for stories about after life and people going to heaven and hell. Basically, after the death of the lower level "I" the "I" finds itself in another world.

We can dig deeper to look at the parallel between the waking and dreaming states. Consider the states of being asleep and dreaming. There is an "I" in the dreaming state, much like the "I" in the waking state. This "I" creates the objects, characters, and circumstances in the dream. As long as the dreams are continuing, the dreamer "I" exists. The moment all dreams cease, or become too much to bear, the dreamer "I" wakes up to the "I" in the waking state. In that case, all the objects in the dream die at once. This is similar to the entire world vanishing at one go, much like the end of a *yuga* (a time period). When we are trying to fall asleep, the waking "I" is present to some extent, controlling dreams to a certain extent. Slowly it loses control, and the dreaming "I" takes over. The situations in the dream become either so bad or so dull that the dreams cease and we wake up. This is exactly what the various *yugas* show.

However, the question now is this: What happens to a particular individual when he or she dies? As we saw from a higher level, life was purely a fiction of his or her own imagination, so the person did not exist in the first place; the person was just a bundle of consciousness or energy, which then disintegrates. The finer question is whether there is anything left in the structure if an individual that continues after apparent death. This leads us to the question of rebirth.

Is Rebirth Possible?

Let us get back to the life cycle of a thought. Assume we have not entertained a thought for a long while. It is devoid of energy and it has "died". We are at the thought level now, not at our level, as the creator of the thought. When a thought dies, does it leave behind any remaining energy? Take a very angry thought for instance. We are angry at someone and we entertained the angry thought for a long time. However, for various reasons (maybe we developed other interesting thoughts that, being more attractive, ignored the first), this angry thought lost our favour and we stopped thinking about it. It ceased to come up in our awareness. But is it really lost? No, it is actually biding its time waiting for more powerful thoughts to either go away or lose energy. Even if the thought is dead, is it not possible for us to recreate the thought and bring it back to life again? If so what was remaining that we brought it back to life?

There are three things in the thought structure. First is the energy associated with it, second are the details, and third are the emotions and linkages attached with it. When a thought gets so drained of energy, it does not show any activity to the other thoughts. It is either classified as dead or in a coma. However, it is possible for us to rekindle the thought by giving it attention. If we give it attention (energy is the equivalent of life) along with the details, we bring the thought back to life. This can be compared to bringing a person back from coma. We may have forgotten the details of many thoughts, but the emotions remain. When we look back at one of these thoughts, the emotions come back and we experience that emotion (anger for instance) in general for no particular reason that we can immediately understand. The present circumstances may be totally different from the circumstances we were in when we previously entertained that thought (this may refer to different phases of our sleep or time period). Now, continuing this scenario with an angry thought, this thought is a carnivorous thought. It is seeking ideal conditions to become a proper structured thought. Soon enough, something comes up that justifies anger. And lo, a new thought is born. Can we take this as the rebirth of an old thought?

Two important questions need to be answered. What happened to the details of the original thought? What is the commonality between both these thoughts? The whole point of the details is that, if the details existed and we brought the thought back to life, it would be like bringing a person back from coma. The commonality between the thoughts was the emotion attached to them.

This is what is being said of the structure of the human body. There are elaborate books on the structure, which is the physical body, the etheric body, the emotional body, and the spiritual body. When we die, the physical body dies. The etheric body, which is fine matter that surrounds the physical body, dies in a few seconds, but the mental and emotional bodies remain. Basically what this means is that the details are lost. So when the emotional and spiritual bodies get energy through the attention and will of the higher source in a different set of circumstances, we have what we call rebirth from the person's point of view. He has his own qualities, which we can call *prarabdha* or karma. The karmas he carries through are dependent on the *vasanas*, which means the residual emotional body. What the thought wants to achieve is dependent on its energy level and its structure. Note that it is not possible for us to determine its course of action, its desires, or its interactions with other thoughts. We can only switch our thoughts on or off. This is similar to the Brahma, Vishnu, and Siva part of us, (the creator, maintainer and destroyer of thoughts) which initiates thoughts, struggles to contain them in harmonious existence, and retires thoughts that are not fitting with the theme. The power of the thought depends upon the energy given to it at the time of its birth. Just as our thoughts determine what they want to do and interact, we also make our own destinies. If we choose a path in accordance with the theme going on currently, we will thrive; otherwise, we will struggle until our energy is exhausted and we die.

However, we need to remind ourselves that, from the higher point of view, it is all one consciousness looking through various structures.

Do Ghosts Exist?

To answer this question we need to first define what we mean by "ghost." The normal understanding is that a ghost is something that is not living. It could be a being after death, but somehow it has the physical powers or the intention to harm us, use us, or kill us. The last part is most important. When I said that there could be a river god or a forest god, we did not react as much as we did when I mention ghosts. The fact that we feel that they somehow want to kill us prevents us from analytical observation; instead we concentrate on what could happen if ghosts were real.

To understand the parallel, let us look at our mental plane and project onto our plane where we want to check if ghosts exist. Next we could also observe our cells and project onto our plane to see if ghosts exist.

As we saw in the mental plane, a thought is nothing but the manifestation of energy, the energy being acquired when we give the thought attention. Now, like true living beings, all thoughts need energy to survive. So either they take energy from the source (which is me, by my attention) or feed on other thoughts to dominate my attention. Now all this is valid while they are alive. When a thought dies, its structure and details are destroyed and it is no longer capable of any action. The other thoughts see this situation as the death of that thought. But a thought, as we saw before, can retain the emotional energy even when it "dies". It remains in some seed form and leaves traces of itself all over the place such that, if I want to, I can reconstruct the thought almost back to its original form. However, if I don't think about the thought, there is no way it could come alive by eating other thoughts. "Dead" thoughts are not capable of doing anything on their own; we must give them our attention if they are to be reborn. Sometimes a variant of the thought may be created, and then that becomes a living thing. This is closely linked to the topic of rebirth, but a thought created as a variant it is a different thought, not a dead thought once more walking around.

Similarly, let us look at the cells in the physical body. When our cells die, they are replaced by new cells. There is no instance in which a cell dead, with no material form, can threaten the already living cells. With this in mind, is it possible for a bundle of energy (a ghost) to retain thoughts so as to extract revenge, for example, as seen in the movies? This bundle of energy is a different bundle from the human physical body. Even if it existed, it would not be possible to do things a physical form could do.

Hence we need to conclude that ghosts, as I've just defined, do not exist.

What could exist, however, are bundles of energy, or traces, which may form part of a theme. For example, you have some angry thoughts because you were angry at something. After the thing or event you were angry at is gone, the anger could remain. All thoughts that came up in this atmosphere would be coloured by anger. You may even revive the original thought, though dead, when you encounter a trigger of some sort later. This is more a case of rebirth rather than a ghost. When a thought is reborn, it follows the same lifecycle as any thought: birth, trying to gather energy (from attention), being choked off by others, and the energy going down until death occurs.

Sometimes a large number of strong thoughts, good or bad, exist in a particular place. It could be a place where many people were killed, or a place where many people have worshipped. When the thoughts die, the energy can remain. When we enter that region, we can be influenced by the energy. That is why temples and some houses of worship have pleasant influences on us. The emotional energy of the thoughts that have occurred there over time remained there. It is said that bricks, wood, crystals, and even metals can absorb the energy and release it to influence us, in a good or bad way.

What Is Time? Is It Absolute or Relative? How Is It Created?

These are very tricky questions. I will give my take on it based on the law.

Let me try to explain time by giving you an example. The earth rotates on its axis once in twenty-four hours. The earth's axis is pointed to a star called the pole star. The axis is tilted with respect to the plane of rotation. However, the axis always points to the pole while going round the sun. As a result different parts of the earth are more directly exposed to the sun during various positions around the sun. So when the earth is in the six-month period during which the North Pole is exposed to the sun (*Uttarayan*) summer days are longer in the northern hemisphere and the reverse in the Southern Hemisphere.

Now consider two people, one at the equator and one near the pole. Also, let us define a unit of work as chopping down one tree. If we define time as that which happens between sunrise and sunset, the person at the equator can chop, say, two trees. The time available for the person at the equator is, say, twelve hours. The person at a higher latitude, whose day extends to, say, eighteen hours, can chop three trees. Let us also assume that there is no other way to measure time except by the sunrise and sunset and hence the unit of time is a day. Now they both know each other well, they meet frequently, and they know that they have the same strength and technique, so the speed of action is the same. They even exchange places and conclude that they can chop more trees at the poles. Then the only explanation is that time goes slower at the poles. Given our current view of time, we know this is false because we have sophisticated quartz watches that advance at the same rate wherever they are on earth. They provide a more accurate record of the passage of time than does the sun. Supposing the watch were to be slower or faster depending on where it was at any given time. We would say that time runs faster or slower there. Thus, time is relative. This is what Einstein meant when he said that, when a train starts moving at the speed or light, the watch slows down, and time goes slowly for people on the train. Notice that the people on the train behave normally and do not feel any "greatness" or elation for having lived longer. There is a beat that is happening inside us, and that beat is like our computer clock speed. The clock speed of a computer is the basic pulse on which all other calculations are based. Any state in the computer can only change with a beat, not in between beats. Thus, if you want to increase the speed of calculations, you need to increase the clock speed.

Now, how do we know time has elapsed?

Here is my theory on time: We have an internal beat, which we are conscious of. Time spent to us is the number of beats of that rhythm. More the beats we notice, more we think time has elapsed. However, our consciousness gets diverted into observing thoughts. To the extent we observe thoughts, we don't count the beats. Thus, when our mind is calm, time seems to go slowly. Or when we have very little thoughts going on in our mind, time seems to go slow. You could try this experiment. Take a watch which has the second hand. Observe the movement of the hand every second. When your mind is calm, you notice the second-hand stops, waits for some time and then moves to the next second. Sometimes if you are very calm, you see the oscillation of the second hand between two seconds too. However, if your mind is full of thoughts, the second hand seems to be moving in a smooth way, no longer do you observe it starting and stopping. This is because our mind takes a snapshot at every pulse of the internal clock beat.

I see that an event has occurred. My mind makes a note or a snapshot of it. It again makes a snapshot of it and notices the change and records it as a second thought. The fact that it has changed, and the fact that I am observing two different snapshots, gives the impression of time passing. I see the first thought, I see the second, and I conclude that something happened in between, and that in between thing is time. To give an example, let's look at the difference between a camera and a video recorder. A camera takes a snapshot as of a particular moment; it has no clue what it was a moment back. It can only tell the picture this instant. Such an instrument does not know time. However, a video recorder outputs a signal once and then, due to a movement of the tape, records and outputs another signal. Since it stores both the states and plays them in succession, the change in the state (as two different signals) gives the impression of time passing. Now, all the signals existed on the tape before and after. However, attention was diverted to one event and then the other, and the difference in the observations give rise to the impression of the passage of time. It is possible for us to pull the tape faster and we get an impression that things are happening quicker. It is possible to play the tape forward and reverse. It is just how we choose the order of events to focus on. Thus in our consciousness we need to have a mechanism to record an event, and in the next beat, record another and compare. This comparison gives us the impression of time. Important thing to remember here is to remember that there is an "I" who is observing these changes of state. Without the beat, the storage of the recording, the observer who compares both, there is no time.

So, if the fundamental beat and the reason for the impression of time are our observations at a particular intervals, if our thoughts are less in number, our time should go slower. Einstein alluded to this when he said, "Put your hand on a hot stove for a minute, and it seems like an hour. Sit with a pretty girl for an hour, and it seems like a minute. That's relativity." It has been my experience that, when I start meditating, frequently I open my eyes to look the clock. (My *Guruji* would not approve I am sure!) In the initial stages, five minutes feel like five hours. When I succeed in quieting my thoughts, after what feels like a long time, I open my eyes and see that only two minutes have gone by! At this rate, I would never reach my intended twenty minutes. The last five minutes, definitely, are the longest. This is because I see a thought, and I see another. Let's say I can recite a mantra ten times in a minute. Now due to the calmness of the mind, I recite it a hundred times and then open my eyes. It should have been ten minutes, but the clock says five minutes. Thus, time is going slower. I read somewhere that Hanuman, a great devotee of Lord Ram, could recite a million "Ram" in a second. Imagine how slowly time would go slowly for him. The calmer I become, the more time slows down.

We could easily think these idea as rubbish. Our experience is that, whether we are observing or not, flowers bloom, people go about their usual ways, and time and tide do not wait for anyone. That is our day-to-day experience. Then what do we mean that time depends on our thoughts? There is a sequence to everything is it not? There are two things we need to remember here. Firstly, we are living in a higher entity's dream world. So, the beat is of that entity which drives time in all the external processes we see. Secondly, this is another dimension like the three co-ordinates of space. Just like an automobile can move only in two dimensions on the ground, a helicopter could move in a third dimension which is go above the ground. The time is a fourth dimension which we can move in.

If I stop thoughts, will time stand still? Then the next question this: Is it possible to go back in time?

To answer this, let us jump back to our dream state. Suppose in my dream I go back to my childhood and go to school only to realize, to my horror, that I have left my assignment at home. The teacher is getting ready to act. The shock is so severe that I wake up. But I quickly realize that I have been dreaming, and I rewind back to the time when I am leaving home. I put in the assignment in my bag and go to class. Now when the teacher asks, the assignment is there in the bag. The characters in the dream may wonder how this person is constantly able to escape in the nick of time. How is he able to go back in time? In the dream state, the time recorder of the events is in our control; we control the level lower than us. What is time to the level below us? It is what we give our attention to, which records the events. The level below us cannot control the flow of events. We can. In other words, for them, their god (us) can go back and forth in time at will. The only way a character in the dream can control time is to come out of the dream and then get back at the required point.

This could be an input to the theory of a time machine. We need to rise above our current level of consciousness and descend to another time. However, if we get out of the dream, the question is, will we decide to get back into the dream?

Parallel Universes, Different Time Speeds

Now that we have come to terms with the fact that the same setup can be seen as living in different ways in the same plane, now to add to the confusion, there are different planes as well! So the same life could actually be doing something else in a different plane.

In the beautiful book by Pandit Rajmani Tigunait called *From Death to Birth: Understanding Karma and Reincarnation page 182*. In this book, he quotes a story from the scriptures about the sage Vashishta and his wife, Arundhati. While they had a complete understanding of life and death, and thus were above them, they wanted to enter the cycle as ordinary mortals and find out where exactly the problem lay so that others could benefit from it. They chalked out a plan: they would enter for two cycles, and if they got caught in the web, the goddess *Saraswati* (the goddess of learning) would come to the rescue. They saw a royal procession and wanted to live as a king and queen. The king, Padma, and queen, Lila, were living a happy life, and Lila did not want her husband to die. Even though she tried to prevent his death, her husband one day fell ill and died. She remembered her connection to goddess *Saraswati* who came and told her that her husband was actually alive and was in the same room. *Saraswati* then took her into another realm but to the same room where the king and queen had been married at sixteen years of age! She saw herself as she used to look. She asked *Saraswati* how this could be possible. Her husband had just died. *Saraswati* said that time moves faster in some planes and slower in others. The goddess explained that there are universes within universes. She then reminded Lila that she was actually Arundhati and took her back to her cottage, which was empty as both Vasishta and Arundati were incarnated. Now they came back to the other realm, where the king and queen were now around eighty years of age, and the king was about to die again. They told him that he was actually King Padma, and this put the king into a lot of confusion as to who he actually was. However, he was brought back to the King Padma realm where he re-entered the body and became alive. Then they both took the help of *Saraswati* and got back to the cottage as Vasishta and Arundathi.

I want to make two points with this story: The first is that there are multiple parallel universes, and we can be in many of them. The second is that time moves differently in different universes. I mentioned that time is actually the distance between thoughts, and so time is actually our mental projection. If time is our mental projection, all of this, while looking complicated, also looks similar to our dreams, does it not? All this seems to be proving what the *Mandukya Upanishad* says – that both the waking state and the dream state are unreal.

How Would God Look Upon Us or Feel About Us?

The answer: God looks upon us as we look down upon our organs or cells. Do you love them? Well you are made up of them, so you want them to be healthy, cheerful, and all that. Are you worried about them? Yes, I hope they get all they want and obey my instructions. Are they all you think about? No. You have other things to do. If the body supports what you want to do, other than general good eating and sleeping, you worry about other things. Another thing – you would expect unquestioned obedience, a sense of duty, and a sense of solidarity with all other cells and organs. If any cells are not acting in the interest of the whole, they may be excised. This is how God feels about us. He will do everything to see that we are happy, up to a point. If we do not act according to the script, he will have us removed. Those who are playing to the script get more energy and attention.

Corollary 1: Even God Has Problems Managing Us!

We are the god of our thoughts in the sense that we create them. But we also have trouble managing them! We derive enjoyment from a few thoughts, and we think that is the end of the matter as we move onto other thoughts. But no, the initial thoughts have lives of their own and come up when they are not needed. They clamour for our attention. We want to concentrate on a few thoughts, but other thoughts won't allow it. The problem only keeps getting worse and worse.

Now, think of another parallel, which is the cells or organs in our body. Without them we are nothing. But we are the entity that decides their fate. We want them to be happy and do their assigned tasks so that we can do what we would like to do. We try to eat well and do the things required for their good upkeep. But the actions we take will never be clear to them. Why do we shave off some hair, which took so much effort to grow? Why are we straining our muscles so hard when we are running for a bus? This cannot be explained to the muscles. We decide to put a few of our organs through stress for some goal that we think justified.

However, we want all our thoughts to coexist harmoniously just as we want all our organs to function in a rule and role abiding way. In fact, we would preach to them if we could, that their greatest goal should be to do their assigned work selflessly – (for our selfish goals!).

I would think that God faces a similar problem. That is why we have *karma yoga* (the path of doing your duty for spiritual growth) and our social responsibilities.

Corollary 2: God Really Does Not Care for Each One of Us as Long as the Theme Is Continuing

I have mentioned this before. I, as Mohan, do not really care which hair cell is living or which hair cell is growing as long as some hair exists on my head. If all my hair cells have a problem, I would worry and try to set it right. So the theme is that I need something in my body, and as long as some cells are managing, I will not bother about it too much. Of course some cells are more important than the others; for example, the cells of the heart and the brain. Also, the importance I give to organs changes. Sometimes I need the muscles to work well, and sometimes I need the brain cells to work well. Each time, I want the least disturbance from the cells that are not so desperately needed. Similarly, God does not bother too much if what he wants is happening in some way or the other. This is a most humbling and disappointing conclusion. We think we are special favourites of God, but that is far from the truth. It is also true that we are unique and are here for a purpose. We will be called upon to do something and at that time we are the only ones who can do that. We could be encouraged by God, however, if we do what he wants us to do, or what we are assigned to do.

Corollary 3: God Will Be Aware of Us Only if Forced To

I read a joke, "I was told that I would be more aware of my body if I start running. Now I am aware of muscles which I never knew existed!" One way of bringing ourselves to the attention of God is cause him pain. The risk is that he may either improve our lot or eliminate us!

So one way of attracting gods attention is to communicate our pain to him. Of course one cell may not attract the attention but together a few can. A pin prick affects only a few cells but gets our entire attention. Similarly many religions organize mass chantings, mass prayers so that a sizable number of people with a similar thought will attract gods attention.

Our thoughts get our attention in a similar way. A few thoughts, or even one thought, come up for review by us. It might be a digested thought as described before, on its way out but just trying its luck at getting your attention. Or it might be a new thought that has been spawned off by other thoughts as another dimension you have not considered. A thought brings along with it an intensity of pain or pleasure in the form of energy. When high energy flows in our minds, it gets our minds' attention. As we shall see later, the only thing we are after is high-energy flows. So either we give this thought more energy, thereby making it stronger so that it can come again, or we stop all other thoughts and give this thought more and more energy. Now this is similar with both a pleasurable thought and a worry, as it is only a definition as to what it is a pleasure or a worry. The after effects of a high-energy outflow is the same.

So the way to get God's attention seems to be to get a few likeminded individuals together and get them to think the same type of thoughts. Now this could be religious or destructive. The constant buildup of mental energy makes the atmosphere conducive to getting the attention of the higher-level being (God), and he is forced to look at what is happening. This partially explains why all evil-minded people are allowed by God to flourish. One frequently asked question is, if God knows a particular person is a bad, why did he not prevent him from existing in the first place? The point is that, when we give our attention to a thought, at that time it is pleasurable. It is only when it gets out of control and is in the process of killing other thoughts that we realize it is time to kill it.

So it is intensity that matters in attracting God's attention. A large number of devotees gathered and chanting a mantra meaninglessly may not attract God's attention, while a few "revolutionists" in a hideout may be getting God's attention. We will discuss this more in detail.

Attracting God's Attention

There are three ways to attract attention:

1. By doing actions that help the current theme

2. By either enjoying something immensely or signalling that it is causing too much pain

3. By disrupting the theme so much that God must take action

To understand the way we should attract God's attention, let us see how our cells would attract our attention. We, of course, want our cells to continue doing their work without much fuss. There are feedback mechanisms that alert us if they are exhausted or hungry or have a problem. Pain or other sensations reach us, and we then take action. Similarly, God would like us to continue doing our duty without much fuss. The system has been set up so that each person doing his or her duty is beneficial to the whole system, and everyone should be enjoying doing his or her duty. One of the positive ways our cells or thoughts can get our attention is to enjoy their existence and communicate that they are enjoying. Pleasant thoughts, for example, occur when our desires are fulfilled or we have a full, satiated stomach. We will immediately try to remove anything that gets in the way of the enjoyment, and let the situation continue. Similarly, whichever theme is being played out currently, if we act according to that, God will direct to us all the energy and circumstances we need.

In all our puranas we see the various *rakshashas* (mythological race of evil people, as opposed to the devas who are supposed to be good) trying to gain attention by various methods, by disrupting the world mainly so that God is forced to act. Ravana was a *rakshasha* who attracted God's attention by developing an intense love for Shiva, and then used up that power to disrupt the world.

To get too much pleasure or pain, we would have to allow a large amount of energy to flow through us, and that would be possible only by lowered resistance to energy flow. This will be a major topic of discussion in future chapters.

What about undertaking actions that would help the current theme of God? That is what is called *Dharma*. If I am running, and my muscles need energy and they are doing a good job, they would receive more glucose from the blood stream. Helping to achieve what God needs will get me attention, which is described as doing one's dharma.

What Is My Dharma (My Duty, My Calling)?

The key to get more "energy" (we will see that this is the most important and joyful thing) or help from God is to understand how the system works and how each entity is helping the others in the world and contributing to it. The system has been set in many ways.

Our duty is special, and only a few of us are actually best placed to do it. This can be compared to the fact that my retinal cells are the only cells in my body best placed to make me see. If they suddenly decided that the blood cells were having all the fun travelling, so they too should start travelling, I would not be able to see. Every cell should do what it is supposed to do, and only that. It should do it well and feel good about it too. So it should be too with ourselves. You may be the only one who can be the parents of your children or the manager in the office or the sportsman on the field or the soldier in the battle. The world has put in a lot of effort to put you there. You cannot back out when you are required.

Our needs are taken care of in a general way, wherein all the people do their duty. For example, if each and every cell, each and every system, works well, I am healthy. However if any set does not do its duty, the entire system collapses, including the cells that thought they could abdicate their responsibilities.

In general, too, in doing our duty, we are given all the help we need. This is not obvious at first. There are mechanisms in place to realize the need and to provide for it. Hunger, thirst, need for sleep are some examples.

In general, doing our duty is pleasurable. Well, not always you may say, but that is the design. Some parts of the task may be strained a bit for a short time, but some other group or the higher level being appreciates the extra effort. More help will come. For example, I pull a particular load on a daily basis, and my muscles ache. I try some muscle-building exercises. The first day is hell. But I drink some protein supplements and exercise further. My focus on and awareness of building my muscles is itself energy, which builds muscle. Not too much later, my muscles are enjoying the activity pulling the same daily load I once struggled.

It could be possible that some cells do not do their duty and try to follow other pursuits. Basically this means that a cell, a group of cells, or an organ are going against the system. To be sure, a corrective mechanism either in the body or through medicine or surgery would be undertaken to redirect that group's endeavours. This means that the test for knowing our duty is not only doing that which is pleasurable, but not doing what causes the system to attack us or cause us pain.

There is also the case of the stem cells. These are like fresh graduates. They are out of college, ready to be moulded to any career. They may look around and decide whether to become a brain cell, or a bone cell. Once they choose, they cannot change. Their choice becomes their Dharma.

The key to all of this is to understand the whole mechanism of how the world is configured, and then to figure out our role and do our duty. Is this all possible by the cells in the body? No. They just follow their instinct and do what is "really enjoyable" to them. Normally, one cell does not kill the other. If that happens, the entire system collapses. Some cells, however, are equipped to kill, and they protect our body. What is the real-world lesson we derive from this? Know your duty and do it. Know your duty by understanding the working of the whole universe, or by doing what is enjoyable to you. The caution to be exercised here is that this should not be taken as a license to follow a libertine path, because the system will cause you pain somewhere along the way. Otherwise, all pleasurable things can and should be done. As I said before, caution is to be exercised here. People who are sensitive to what is really a pleasure or pain in the long run, and good for all things considered, should question this path. The rest can learn from scriptures or other authoritative texts.

How should we behave in our god's world? Well, our behaviour should mimic the way we want our thoughts, and our cells to behave. We will be at mental peace when thoughts come up for your enjoyment, present their case, and make way for others to shine, is that not correct? When we want them to come, they should, and when we don't want them, they should go away into the background. They should allow other thoughts to come and play out their part. In fact, if we want one particular thought, all thoughts should help that thought. Any thought that does not allow that should be banished and killed if necessary. We actually want each and every thought to behave exactly as we created it to. We want it to enjoy itself, fulfil its best potential in the allotted time. So, in short, the duty of a thought is to come into existence, do what it was created to do, have a great time, and make a graceful exit. That is exactly what we should be doing in our lives. If we want to have the thought for a longer time, we give that thought more energy. Similarly, if God wants us to do more, he will prolong our lives.

How we should conduct ourselves and how God will help us along the way has been laid out clearly as "*yogas*"; namely karma yoga (doing our duty without worrying about results), upasana yoga (thinking about god as a particular form to the exclusion of all ese), bhakti yoga (devotion to god in all repsects), and gnana yoga (knowledge of all this theory of god and your true self). Mind you, these are all linear, and we have to progress from one to the other.

Imagine we are in the middle of action, say for example, on the battlefield. If we were to go to God for help, he would say, "I understand, but please work harder. I need you to work harder." In that case we do our best. This is karma yoga. If it is some problem in my body, only he can send the right medicine to set right. This can be compared to Krishna saying he will come again and again to set right things. We can only signal to him that things are not good and wait for his intervention. This is bhakti yoga. If we are the problem, we need to understand the whole thing and act in harmony with others and realize that we are part of the whole. This is gnana yoga. How do we determine the current situation with regard to a problem we are having? We have to look around for signs. We have to understand how things are so we can live in harmony and understand our role in it.

Fate and Self-Effort

This is another topic that inspires people to swing from one extreme to another, and the truth is usually somewhere in between.

Certain people say that everything is predestined by God; his will is what will be done, so why should we do anything at all? Other people say there is nothing like a God; we do everything ourselves, and hence self-effort is the only way. A few others play it safe and say God will help those who help themselves; their goal is not to make God angry in case he does exist!

Let us use the Law of Correspondence here, as we discuss the fact that I am the god of the levels below me (the parts of my body). Should the heart do its duty by self-effort or should it give up saying that it's god (me) who will take care of everything? On one hand, it is not possible for me to do the work of each and every organ and each and every cell. I have other things to do as well. I would strongly encourage each organ and cell to do what it should do to the best of its capacity. On the other hand, to say that the heart can do the work of others as well as its own is also not right. In fact, I take great care to exercise and eat the right foods to keep the heart healthy. Everything that the heart needs, I provide. The heart may think that it gathers what is available around it, but there is a huge system in place that ensures it gets what it needs. And so it is with each and every organ of the body. If there is a problem, I intervene. If they communicate that there is a problem (through pain or illness), I intervene. But I am not going to supervise each organ or cell. This is exactly how God looks down on us.

What Is My Karma (fate)?

Probably this is a most misunderstood concept. The extremes are diverse. At one end, we say that it is all fate and we leave everything to our fate. At the other end, we disregard fate and believe in self-effort only. Many writings and theories are available on the theory of karma. Of course the Bahagavad Gita gives us the famous sentence that we have rights based on the karma we do, not on the fruits of the karma. But the general misunderstanding of karma is fate.

How do we apply the Law of Correspondence to the theory of karma?

Let's return to the waking state as we go into the dream state. We are at the stage where a thought has some energy and it is maintaining its status with that energy. For this purpose, we will say it has "life". Now, given its type of energy, it wants to do something that will attract more energy. For this it wants to draw our attention to itself. But it is in an environment where other thoughts have their own energies and agendas. As a thought, its main aim is to get more energy, not give out energy to others. It also aims to store energy for future use and do what is pleasurable. Now, other thoughts also want to do the same. Every thought, when it spends energy, is noticed by others. Others with similar agendas may help this thought. Those opposed will push it away. In general, the result of the complex interaction is a sum of all the interactions, which is too hard to predict. To add to this confusion, I (as a higher-level being) have my own agenda and want to encourage a few types of thoughts. I would give more energy (attention) to those with the current theme and shut out others. When I give attention to a thought, my awareness of it depends totally upon what it has accumulated so far and the linkages to other thoughts. Accordingly I encourage or discourage it.

The thought has built up some type of energy like love, joy, anger, hate, greed, and so forth. Depending on the theme, it may attract more friends or enemies; it may also attract my attention, positive or negative. This built-up energy as well as the connections determine its future. This is loosely called fate or karma. Karmas themselves are of three types, but explaining that would be a digression.

Now, every thought is fully capable of realizing what works in the current environment, and it is capable of conducting itself accordingly. It could mean junking other energies not required at this time. This is self-effort, which can change the fate of a thought. The self-effort could result in a positive or negative outcome depending on the environment at that time.

One thought that is actually doing good to other thoughts, in general being a good citizen, may not be in favour temporarily. However, it will bloom once the environment becomes more conducive to what it has been doing. We have to realize that the inimical thoughts are actually being enjoyed by the higher level for the time being. They will be killed when they go out of control.

Now, a thought builds up energy in a structure, which will make it behave in a particular way in the future, as long as it is active. It builds linkages with other thoughts, and its fate is more or less decided by this complex interaction, which it itself created in the past. For example, I want to own a certain car. That thought attracts other thoughts, which provide ideas as to how that could be possible – how to buy it, where to buy it, how to get loan for it, and so on. When I give attention to the sheer pleasure I would get by driving the car, the other thoughts become enlivened. Now, suddenly, if the main thought – the one about enjoying the car – decides to take some rest, do you think the other thoughts will allow that to happen? The loan thought keeps reminding me to go and buy the car. Similarly, the other linked thoughts push their way to the forefront of my mind. The main thought is now stuck with its own "fate", no doubt created by itself. This is called karma. Now, even if the main thought "dies", the energy and the linkages remain. The type of energy surrounding it reflects joy. Now a new thought comes up and absorbs this energy, and the theme may be now to enjoy a new house. Thus, the karma of the previous birth is carried over. All the linkages become activated and now become attached to a new home rather than a new car. Similarly, when an angry thought dies, it will give birth to another angry thought. Karma gets carried forward.

Now, how does this correspond to ourselves? There is nothing material we carry forward after our death. Just as the thought in the above example carried forward a theme, we also carry forward a theme, which will play out in a future birth. These are *vasanas* or tendencies, which linger around us and get carried forward to the next birth. Our past vasanas become us.

Why Are These Things Happening to Me? How Do I Change Them?

What is the use of all this theory if it does not help me solve problems in my day-to-day world?

We must learn to differentiate between a problem and normal stress.

My brain cells may be stressed for various reasons. If I am writing an exam, they'd better be stressed! Or there may be some chemical problem that could cause the brain cells to be under stress. Or some cells may be working against the theme, so the work at hand is becoming more difficult. If it is the first case, I would ask my brain cells to work harder! If it is the second case, I need the cells to tell me, by giving a headache, so that I am alerted and take some medicine to set right the problem. In the third case, my brain cells should behave better and be organized and not start off on a theme on their own, but should work in harmony with the other cells.

In short, we can understand why things are the way they are only if we are on a higher level. Until then, we can only follow our roles to the extent possible, and wait for help. It could also be that we are going against the current theme. As someone said, if all the traffic is driving right at you, you must be driving in the wrong lane.

Why Is Desire So Good?

Ask people why they are doing what they are doing, and they will tell us for joy and happiness. They may even say for everlasting and intense joy. Hence many people are after many things, but these things are specific to that person and are not interchangeable. Even to the same person, one object does not give everlasting joy. In fact, the logic goes something like this: Joy is so difficult to get, this thing is also so difficult to get, so this thing, when attained, should give us joy. And they are right most of the time.

This must be one of the most important questions for humankind. Since the beginning of time, desire has been the basic reason for family and society. Humans have expended a lot of energy on desire; they have tried to control it, to channel it, to ridicule it, to condemn it, to worship it, and so forth. But nobody could ignore it. It has been the reason we see all the crimes against women, and all heartbreak, but also it is the reason for strong family ties.

Of course, if we don't understand desire, we are not going to be able to control it in any way.

Why is desire so good? Or, what in desire is so good? These are questions that need to be answered for the benefit of humanity. Can the Law of Correspondence help us here? Yes, of course! The points are subtle, but I would draw parallels with electric and magnetic fields of all things!

In fact, in the puranas, we learn how the universe was created and the difficulties faced when desire did not exist. The story of Adam and Eve and the Hindu puranas talk about desire and how central it is to the universe.

It is said that *Brahma* (the creator) created a few sages, like Narada and Sanat-Kumaras, and hoped that his job was done because they would create other beings. These sages had a great deal of energy because they were the mind-children of Brahma himself. Since they had so much energy, they did not want anything else, and because they were so happy where they were, they spent all their time in meditation. Brahma expected that they would procreate and populate in the world. Since this did not happen, Brahma created a mechanism that released a high amount of energy during sex. The energy rush was so pleasurable that everyone wanted the experience again and again, and they wanted it to last forever. Brahma then created all the other beings with this desire.

When there were fewer people in the world, the amount of energy available was great, and the production of energy was not a problem. This can be compared to our thoughts. Each thought is more intense when we have very few thoughts. When we have too many thoughts, the energy available is divided, and less energy is available for each thought. The energy required for pleasure is, however, fixed. Now, when we are weak, it is not possible to easily release such an amount of energy. Hence, energy is allowed to build up just as energy is built up in a capacitor. This done by increasing awareness in all areas we know of – the mind, the intellect, the emotions, and of course in many parts of the body. The mind starts to become intensely aware of a thought. Now, just as food is the mechanism that provides energy to the body, attention is the mechanism that provides energy to thoughts. Hence, the mind starts to build up energy. Next, the mind is aware of the intense feeling in the body, and more energy builds up. All this pent-up energy is released in an instant. This is the intense energy rush that every living thing craves for.

So sex is very good because of the energy rush. It is not due to any physical being, object, or thought. The same is true for any desire. Things become attractive to us relative to the amount of energy we build on that particular topic. If we talk about food, the food tastes better. Imagine thinking of a special meal all week, then making a reservation at a restaurant. Imagine the immense rush of energy when the food just melts in your mouth, just as you thought it would.

When I hear of all the cases of rape or of people lusting for certain other people, I feel sad. That is because the person is not craving a particular person or thing, but for the energy rush associated with connecting with that person or thing. However, this is like a camera flash. There is a burst of energy after which the batteries take some time to recharge. However, what everyone wants is a continuously glowing flash.

So, desire gives us joy because of the rush of energy. As long as energy is flowing, we feel joy. The larger the energy flow, the larger the joy.

Normally we do not have enough energy to produce joy, and especially to produce joy that will last for a long time. Hence, we need to build up the energy and then release it. We wrongly associate the container in which we build up the energy as the cause of joy. One thing to note is that if the thing had an intrinsic joy in it, all of us must find it enjoyable. However, each one of us think a different thing is enjoyable. Even the same person will not find the same thing enjoyable on different days. Also, the same thing if taken in larger quantities will not give us more joy, but there is a diminishing return of joy.

To build up the pressure of the energy, we require a container. If the container is a physical one like a balloon, we could store and release energy in small quantities, as we would enjoy the small pleasures of life. Jokes, and some harmless pastimes are like small balloons which can build up small pressures. However, the strong containers are family bonds, love, revenge, gambling, sex, horror stories, and movie jealousies. The strong containers are all connected to the ego in some way. Will I lose a lot of money? Will I get caught? Will I die? A great deal of fear is involved. These build up enormous energies. All the seven sins are strong containers. If we combine two or three, we get an even bigger buildup! Remember, scandal and gossiping are all containers in which energy can build up. The Roman games, which involved gladiators and chariots, always offered the crowds the possibility that someone would be killed. This was an extreme way of building up the energy pressure.

The Bhagavad Gita presents a clear sequence of events. First there is a desire, a longing; we think that if this thing becomes ours, we would be happy. We then build up energy on that thing by constant effort including fantasizing about it, remembering it, and researching it. If that thing is not attained, we become angry. Anger leads to delusion, and delusion leads to confusion between right and wrong, and finally this leads to the ruin of the person. We have a choice at each stage to stop it. The easiest, of course, is to stop it at the desire stage. If we do not stop there, it isn't too difficult to stop at the buildup stage. Once the energy is built up, however, it is very difficult to control the situation, much less stop it.

Why and how does sex produce life? Let us look at the parallel to sex in the mental plane. Two opposite type of mental energies – corresponding to the male and the female, which is the intellectual and emotional – get together very intensely. They pour a great deal of energy into this union. The idea takes place, and there are many issues to be resolved before we strike the "a-ha" moment. This is when there is a rush of energy and all our energies reach a saturation point. After that, we experience a blank moment with nothing but peace and exhilaration. How long this lasts depends totally upon how much energy we put into it in the first place, both intellectually and emotionally. In order for an idea to be born, intense energy must be built up and released in a short while. Similarly, I believe that, for a life to be born, intense energy has to flow into the physical system, which is a combination of the male and female.

Well, all this theory is fine you may say. Should we then not pursue joy? Granted, that the joy is not in the thing, but we don't know any other way. At least that moment when the anticipated food just melted in the mouth we were happy. Are we saying we stop striving for these brief moments of joy too? Are we then to lead a joyless life being afraid of sadness for the most part?

So the question is, how can we experience the energy rush without the desire? How do we keep the energy flowing always? Can we avoid the effort required to build up the energy? Can we build up the energy without an object of attention?

It is possible to experience large energy flows with little effort and no object of attention. However, before we learn how, we need to investigate some more concepts.

Energy Flow Is the Most Enjoyable Thing

As we saw in the previous section, energy flow is the fundamental thing sought after in the universe. In my view, joy can be defined as flow of energy within us. This is true in different planes as well.

For example, electrical energy flows from higher "potential" to lower potential. Magnetic flux is the amount of magnetic lines of force passing through an area. Heat is also the energy flow from a higher temperature to a lower temperature. Similarly, light energy and kinetic energy are "something in flow", or, as Einstein put it, condensed energy, or "matter". In fact, there are many books about how the whole world is nothing but energy. Matter is supposed to be condensed energy waves. There are finer and finer vibrations, and the interplay between all this is what we see as the world. In fact, we ourselves are energy. It is said that Shiva is the material aspect and *Shakti* is the energy. Actually they are one and the same. When energy is converted to matter or vice versa, they become thoroughly intermingled. It is the interplay between these that we see as the world. If there were only matter, there would be no life. If there were no energy, there would be no world as we see now. In fact, a being is born when energy decides to enter one structure, and there is death when energy leaves the structure. The important point is that it is the flow, not the energy itself, that is sought after and spectacular. The energy may be present in the battery, but it does not excite anybody until it flows through a circuit.

We can see very interesting parallels in energy flow and conversions. In fact, the hermetic law can see some sort of a proof in how energy flows and behaves in various planes, and the similarity is the proof of the hermetic law. We know how to convert some forms of energy to other forms; for example, heat, light, electricity, and magnetic power can in some way or another be converted one to the other. We don't have a mechanism to convert mental energy to any other form, so we are not aware how to tap it directly.

We are familiar with the normally occurring forms of energy such as heat, light, magnetism, and electricity, so we don't need to elaborate on them here. Rather, we should look at other forms of energy and see how they are similar to all other energies. For example, in the mental plane, we have awareness as energy. *Kundalini* (loosely defined as nervous energy) is also a form of energy, which is residual energy. This is the energy remaining after all material has been created from the total energy in the world. It is actually the residual energy, which can be used to run the world; otherwise, everything would be inert matter. It is important to note that all life is the flow of energy, and the choice is actually left for the energy to determine what it thinks is an interesting case to explore. We will see later on how this means that we should let the (female) energy decide which (male) structure it chooses. Thus awareness entering into matter can also be defined as life. Awareness exists in a frog. The energy experiences how the environment looks to a frog. It also experiences how the environment looks to a snake. It also experiences, at the same time, how a frog and a snake feel when the snake is eating the frog. Awareness is aware of all the millions of experiences. This is what is described as "that with a *Sahasrakshi*, or thousand eyed (countless eyes)" in various *stotras* (hymns of praise).

Again, we come back to the concept that it is the flow of energy that matters, but not energy itself that is enjoyable. Energy, which is simply potential, is useful, but is not interesting to the observer or for the higher-level being. This is true for mechanical energy because, unless something is moving – or in electrical energy, unless there is a flow of current – nothing happens. This flow of energy also happens in our bodies and minds, and later we will see that this is exactly what every living being is after. In general, the higher the energy flow, the higher the enjoyment, until there is burnout.

Energy flow is also the preferred state of energy. Consider a magnet. In a circular magnet, or a U-shaped magnet with a metal piece between its poles, magnetic energy flows within the magnet. In other words, a "circuit" of energy flow is formed. If this circuit is broken, the magnet tries to make it up somehow and even physically exerts a force to make it happen. For example, if we cut the circular flow, we will get two parts, one in which the energy is flowing out, and one in which the energy is flowing in. One is called the north pole, and the other the south pole. It is similar with a positive electrical charge and a negative electrical charge. They are all trying to complete the circuit for the energy flow, and hence there is actually a force of attraction between the poles. The force even tries to induce the environment to complete the circuit; for example, an iron piece will become magnetized to allow the circuit to complete. We see here that there is a part where the energy flows out (called north pole in magnetism, positive charge in electricity) and a part where the energy gets back in. The system tries to complete the circuit, thus giving rise to the notion that "opposites attract". We see the phenomenon as opposites attracting each other, but actually energy is trying any means to complete the flow. Any outward flow of energy could be called the male aspect, and a receiver the female aspect (this is purely an arbitrary definition).

There are all types of circuits, big and small. Delicate structures need small flows to exhibit something interesting. Larger flows, obviously, need larger flows to show more spectacular results. In our mental planes, we enjoy more energy flow. I have included a long chapter on this later, but here we can say that the more the energy flow in our mind, the more we enjoy. In fact, all living beings in our plane struggle to get more energy. In our mental planes, our thoughts struggle to get energy (our attention), and by extrapolation, above us, we can understand that gods are also struggling to get more energy. It is all about *Shakti* – power.

Why Do We Need New Movies Every Year? Why Is Stereo Sound So Good?

Every time a great movie is made, it is proclaimed as the best movie ever. Not only that, but some say that a better movie cannot be made. Yet we want to watch a new movie every day. It is not only movies; it is the same with a new joke, some new gossip, a new dish to eat, and so forth. If a movie is so great, should we not get the same rush of joy every time we see it? Even the greatest fan will not be able to see it more than a dozen times. And when we see a movie the second time, we enjoy the parts we missed the first time. Why is it that we crave something new every time? It has to do, of course, with energy flow. But there is more to it.

Our brain/mind is the valve that allows energy to go through our body. I alluded to this when we talked about the energy flow we experience after we exercise. When the mind or brain is not thinking anything new, it does not need any energy, so it allows only a small amount to flow through. In fact, it may not allow anything at all and may use the energy that is already stored. All this only makes us tired.

However, when new material is presented, different parts of the brain light up. There is so much to be analyzed! In the movie, we need to understand the emotions, the story line, and the logic all at the same time. And every good director builds the tension. As we saw, it is the energy release that is important. So to release a large amount of energy, even for a short time, we need to build the attention of the brain. The brain's attention now is focused on the screen. What could happen next? Will the hero escape? How? Many cannot hold the suspense for long, so they cannot hope to build a vast energy flow and hope for a release. So the writer and director must find a perfect balance that builds the energy of an average person and then releases it at one go. That is why comedians keep their best jokes for the last. In fact, any joke is funnier once the audience members have built up sufficient energy. Jokes are funny because they build up energy and release it in that moment when something unexpected happens.

Now suppose we see the "best movie". We loved the twists and turns. However, when we see the movie again, we remember all those twists and turns so there is no buildup of energy in our brains, unless we are able to observe something new in the scene or plot. If there is no energy buildup, there will be no rush of energy when the climax comes.

It is the same with stereo sound. It seems that, with mono sound (that which comes from one speaker), only one part of the brain lights up, and a moderate energy flow occurs. The sound may be of the best quality, but the brain does not give it much importance. When the sound is stereo, more parts light up, as there is much more to analyze now. Which sound is coming from the left side, which is coming from the right side? Oh, the drummer is running from here to there. The car is coming on the left and now it has vroomed to the right. This simulates real-life hearing so the brain gives it more importance. This energy flow gives us more thrills.

Why Do We Laugh? Why Are Jokes Funny?

In a joke, there is a buildup of our attention. We listen raptly to the story, and the energy builds up within us. At the right moment, when we are being led in one direction, suddenly our thinking is exposed to another direction, and we sort of slip and break our step, which results in the release of energy. Now the "funniness" of the joke entirely depends upon how much energy was built up. If the topic was something that we have thought about, or it was a vexing problem, the pent-up energy is great, and we end up on the floor laughing. If the topic was unknown or distasteful, our minds (remember, it is the valve that allows energy in) does not build up energy, and we don't understand what is so funny. Our minds achieve the appropriate mindset when we know we are going to listen to a known comedian, or a known series of jokes, or when someone announces that he or she is going to tell a joke. We buildup energy in advance and in anticipation. Sometimes we remember the previous jokes about the comedian and this allows the energy to build up. That is why good comedians don't tell their best jokes in the beginning. The same jokes that would just have seemed silly at the beginning of the show, when told in the end of the show, evoke the greatest laughter because people have been sufficiently primed. I read a story once about a boy who was used to hearing a joke every day from his uncle during breakfast. This was almost like a ritual. Slowly, he started to expect a joke – any joke – and he used to relive the previous jokes. So even before the uncle started speaking, the boy was all ready to burst out laughing. When the uncle cracked the silliest of jokes, the boy would roll on the floor in laughter. When the uncle told the same jokes to others, they could not understand what was so funny.

It is the rush of energy that makes us feel joyful, causing us to laugh. Some people can build up a lot of energy. Notice them. They can concentrate for longer times and absorb more material. It is like a balloon. If your balloon is small and hard, no matter how hard and how long you blow, it will only expand so much. Larger, softer balloons can absorb more. They also discharge more. It is the discharge of energy that is enjoyable. Those who have little ability to concentrate can build up only so much and they can laugh only so much. It appears as if, even to enjoy life, we need concentration.

Male and Female Energies

Though energy is the same, we can see some differences in the flow of energy. Energy by itself cannot achieve anything. It needs structure. It is the flow of energy that results in a phenomenon. This is what is observed, and everything is for the amusement of the observer, as we have been saying. Thus an electric plug is boring, and a TV is boring until energy flows through it. A merging of the structure (the TV) and the energy (electricity) is required to make anything of interest.

This is symbolized in Hinduism as Shakti and Shiva. Shakti is pure energy, and it is always asking Shiva to get involved so that something interesting can occur. Shiva provides the structure. Either without the other is of no use.

This happens in our world too. Mothers want their children to derive energy from them and achieve greater heights. I may sound chauvinistic here, but I am talking about the energies and personality types rather than actual people. Anyone who provides structure to the relationship is acting as the male energy; for example, the father providing the physical house and the physical food and clothing. It is not possible for a home to exist with only one without the other.

However, we should note that both wait for the other and cannot and should not force the issue. This is the equivalent of a rape. A structure can be made, but the energy will come and decide if it is worth entering that structure for a good result. If not, it will look for a better structure. There can be no force here, and if the structure is well made, the energy will flow. If there is no structure, energy will keep pushing the material to form one.

This is true in our dream world as well. The existing thoughts create a situation that they think is interesting. You give attention to what you think is interesting. This is Shakti flowing through Shiva in the dream world. If any attempt is made by the structure to capture your attention, at some stage you will break it. If you cannot, that would not result in a good environment or world. It is the same in the real world too. If the female energies are forced or constrained, we will have a suboptimal world. The male energies have to make a good structure and wait for the female energies to enter; if they don't enter, the males must make a better one.

All living things are living because of the flow of energy. The aim of all living things – mental, physical, virtual – is to increase the flow. If flow is a trickle, there would be a mechanism to build a storehouse of energy and give it out in a burst. This is what makes jokes funny; this is what makes desire so good. The flow increases when either a higher pressure is applied, there is less resistance to flow, or both. This is the foundation for the theory of meditation.

The Law as Applied to Meditation

There are various types of meditation prescribed, and often quarrels break out about which is the "best type". It is also said that what is suitable is dependent on the disciple. However, unless we truly understand what it is, why is it required, and how it works, we cannot make much headway.

Let us apply the Law of Correspondence to meditation. Again, suppose in the dream world, "I", the observer in the dream, am observing that I am dreaming. Until the time I was lost in the dream, I was helpless; the moment I realize that I am the dreamer, I become all powerful. There is nothing I cannot do in the dream and nothing left to be achieved in the dream. How can we reach the stage where observe ourselves?

Most of the processes in meditation techniques are spent in cleaning up the mind, or in decreasing the internal resistance of the mind. It is not possible to have an hour of meditation without leading a simple waking life in the other times. The aim is to reduce the thoughts and not to accumulate more thoughts. Many ingenious ways exist, so we have a considerable number of choices, all depending on what suits us personally.

One aspect of meditation is mandatory for all techniques: observing yourself doing something. Shree Rajneesh, also known as Osho, developed many techniques, all of which involve observing ourselves doing routine things like walking, thinking, dancing, and the like. The very act of observing oneself stops the flow of thoughts and results in deep meditation. If the technique also combines observing while asking oneself who is this "I" who is observing and what I am observing is different from me, the meditation becomes deep in a very short time. It is possible to overdo this part. So many techniques start with the chanting of a mantra, at first out loud, and then silently in the mind. If you observe yourself chanting the mantra, and you abruptly stop the chanting, then you are observing yourself doing nothing. For a short moment of time, there is stillness. Extending this stillness is the aim of all the techniques. When you are observing yourself doing nothing, you suddenly wake up. You, as the meditator, have no control over this waking up. It happens in an instant. It is like waking up from sleep. You must just wait for it to happen. People call it waiting for God's grace, but it is like our mental state just before waking up. Suddenly, in a flash, you are awake. If we wake up from this world, we call it attaining liberation, and we enter a new world.

Why and How Meditation Works

To understand how meditation works, let us look at how we work and derive energy in the physical plane. There is one subtle point to notice. Whenever we work with awareness we don't feel tired. For example, when we climb the steps with complete awareness of the stress and strain in each and every muscle, we don't feel tired after the exercise. When we mechanically do something, for example climbing the stairs, while preoccupied with some worry, we have given very little attention to the activity, and hence whatever energy was stored in the muscles is exhausted, and this leaves us exhausted too.

We normally assume that energy comes from the food we eat or the air we breathe. I think that is not the whole truth. The entire process of digestion is to just keep the raw materials at the right place and time; it must be near the cells ready for energy release. Awareness plays a very large part in us doing anything. The mind also plays an important part. This is a topic that needs to be elaborated upon later.

We can use this principle in a positive way too. Try one of the following experiments. Close your eyes and visualize yourself trying to push your red, heavy luxury car. You are huffing and puffing. Feel the strain in your legs and hands. Or visualize yourself walking up the stairs you normally climb every day. Feel the strain in your legs. Look around and see the familiar things. Notice the stress and strain in all your leg muscles. Visualize yourself now running up the stairs. Feel your legs go up one after the other.

In either of these exercises, you were "aware" of the effort in your body. This automatically brings in energy. (How and why the energy comes in will be elaborated upon later.) But you have not actually pushed the car or climbed the stairs! So your body feels refreshed and full of energy.

I fractured a bone in my leg. The initial recovery went well, but full recovery was taking a long time. I was experiencing a small nagging pain in the tendons. Everyone told me that tendons take time to heal. One day I decided I'd had enough of this. I did the mental stair climbing exercise. In fact, I had difficulty in climbing down real stairs, so I visualized myself running down virtual stairs. I saw remarkable progress in my healing in just a day.

The mind plays a major part in the release of energy. I read somewhere that there was a woman whose kids got trapped under a car. With a superhuman effort, she lifted the car and got the kids out. Later she was told that it was not possible for anyone her size to lift the car, and she agreed. She could no longer move the car with all her effort. My theory is this – the mind decides how much energy is to be absorbed through awareness from somewhere (we are surrounded by an energy field). Energy is then released to whatever extent is required at a given time. When the mind decides that only so much energy can be released and hence only so much output can be achieved, then only that much level of result will be seen. The world record for the 100-meter dash was ten seconds for many centuries, but after the first man broke it, many others also broke it easily. The mind decides that more energy release is possible, and hence that output is made possible.

In the experiments I've described, the trick is to make the mind believe that it is *really* pushing the car or climbing the stairs. If our minds believe that it is all make believe, no amount of daydreaming will release any energy into the body. There are exercises that ask us to concentrate on each set of muscles, clenching them and releasing them for energy. This uses the same principle, which is intense awareness of a part of the body while not actually spending energy. When we actually push a car or climb steps, awareness brings in energy and muscles spend out the energy so the energy is cancelled. If we are not aware, no energy comes in and we get tired or our muscles experience pain. In fact, pain comes because the muscles need our attention so that energy can come to them.

What Is Meditation?

We have just seen that energy can be built up on a few thoughts. This gives the thoughts more energy. Then the release of that energy is a joyful experience.

In that case, our efforts should be to reduce the number of thoughts we have. The mind, like the flow of energy is difficult to control if the current is very high. Various techniques, lifestyles are prescribed by various religions to reduce the thoughts we have. The usual suspects, the seven deadly sins, and almost all delicious and salacious things have been classified as sin, and hence to be reduced. Sometimes this can be counter-productive. However, this is a difficult art and needs techniques and pracitce.

There is an interesting parallel in the physical plane. It seems that our minds are valves that determine how much energy is to be allowed into the body and its cells. This is to prevent under or over absorption of energy into the body. Thus, if you are pushing a car, your mind realizes that a large amount of energy is required, and it acquires it for the body. As you actually push the car, the levels of energy input and output balance each other. If you do any activity without involving your mind, the cells expend energy without getting input; hence you feel tired. It seems when you exercise while looking at your muscles in the mirror, the muscles grow faster. If you jog with your mind on your music, you get tired. I heard a gym instructor say that people who use cardio equipment with music plugged into their ears, or while attending to phone calls show slow results. The mind has to be involved to show results. In the above example, if we trick our mind that we are pushing the car by visualizing that we are pushing the car, even without actually pushing it, we will be full of energy.

As we are aiming for a rush of energy for joy, we look at another parallel: how electrical energy flows through wires. According to Ohm's law, for a given electrical pressure (voltage) we get a current flow that is inversely proportional to the internal resistance of the wire: V/I=R in the familiar Ohm's law. In simple terms, if the internal resistance of the wire is high, we get low current, and if the voltage applied is higher we get more flow of current in the same wire. If we take a small cell and connect a 1.5 V bulb to it by two wires, we get a small glow. Nothing spectacular. Now if we remove the bulb and just short the cell by holding just the wires to the cell, we get red-hot wires and a burnt finger. Even though the cell is a small energy source, we get high currents. So one way to increase the energy flow to get high current levels is to decrease the internal resistance.

In the wires, the resistance is caused by impurities that block the flow of current. Pure metals conduct better, but still produce resistance due to impurities here and there. It is possible to have extremely pure metals, with regular crystal structure, which behave as superconductors. This essentially means that, even with very small voltages, they produce large currents that last for a long time.

In the mental plane, our undigested thoughts are the resistance to the energy flow. As soon as an energy flow occurs, it encounters some thought and is dissipated. So we get a rush of energy when our minds are generally free of thoughts, as we saw in the above section.

We have seen some people who are generally happy at the slightest of things, and for a longer time. Children are like that. These people have low internal resistance.

We should not conclude that internal resistance in the wire or in the mind is necessarily a bad thing. For one thing, it can never be totally eliminated, and sometimes it is the very reason for our enjoyment. The bulb glows only due to the resistance, and the mind functions only because of flow our thoughts.

The next step is to increase the voltage. For many of us, it takes a lot of hard work to get rid of our thoughts, and it is often counterproductive. We think more of the very thoughts we want to forget! In fact, we have great attachment to those thoughts. So, we look at how to increase the voltage. But this is dangerous. The heat in a wire is proportional to resistance. In other words, high resistance means higher heating. If in the mental plane we try to energize our minds without decreasing our internal resistance, we get a big headache or damage ourselves. We are generally unaware of how to increase the voltage. But since we are surrounded by energy, the question is more about how to connect ourselves to that energy rather than the availability of high-energy sources. Please note that the heating is proportional to the square of the voltage in the formula $E = v^2/R$. Higher pressure in the mind can be achieved by the chanting of mantras for example. These words contain potent powers, and they either generate energy or connect to the energy sources in the cosmos. Either way, they energize us, and either way, the voltage goes up. However, as I mentioned before, if we increase voltage and the resistances are large, the current will be low and the joy will be low and will be dissipated almost immediately. However, this is a great improvement over a weak energy source. Ideally we should do both – increase voltage and decrease internal resistance.

So what are the ways we can decrease the blockages in our minds? By reducing the number of thoughts and the internal structures. Easier said than done! Firstly, we don't want to lose the thoughts that we have so painstakingly built. Who would want to drop his or her dearest thoughts in one go? Secondly, we don't have the technique to drop specifically what we want to forget; for example, that insult we received a few years back. This is where almost all of the religious texts have concentrated their efforts. All religious texts provide lists of dos and don'ts. The dos are spectacularly boring because all the "good" things are prohibited. As it is said, all the "good" things in life are illegal, immoral, or fattening! Why these are illegal or immoral is another topic. Here I am asking the question: What is the benefit of shunning the illegal and immoral things. Actually, if the reason we need to do this were explained and understood properly, there would not be a need for discipline, and everybody would voluntarily do the right thing all the time. The desirable things create a network of thoughts in our minds. This increases the internal resistance to the energy flow in our minds. Even if we were to obtain joy by indulging in these things, it would be a feeble joy. Even if we experience joy in the first round, thoughts would be added (we would want to experience the same with some variations), and we would experience the Law of Diminishing Returns. What gave us joy in the first round would start heating up after some time. We would drop this headache and find a different thing, and endlessly do this.

That is why there is a good reason to follow the way of life as all religions have laid it out – not because they said so, but because by following them we decrease the thoughts in our minds, which leads to greater joys for the things we actually do. It is like increasing the focus on things you do by doing only a few things. If this principle is understood – that the aim is to reduce the internal resistance of our minds (reduce the number of thoughts) so that we may experience greater joy – then we will do this voluntarily rather than because someone asked us to. One example is a requirement that we do our duty without worrying about the result. Having no expectation for the result prevents mental buildup. Another example is "do your duty and leave the rest to God." This again prevents mental buildup because we have left the result to God. If you don't like these methods and injunctions and you have a better method, go ahead and use it!

A corollary of Ohm's law is that current will try to find the path of least resistance. Thus, if we have multiple resistances in parallel, the current in each will depend upon its own internal resistance. As we can see in our houses, the voltage is the same for all appliances, and the current consumed by them and the effects they create are entirely their own constructions. Larger flows of current occur in those with lower resistance.

We can now look at other energy flows. These are not easily observable, but they are well known. Actually, the Law of Correspondence works well when we compare electrical and magnetic flows. For example, magnetic lines of force will go through more magnetic material. The amount of lines of force going through an area is defined as magnetic flux, and the magnetic intensity is defined as flux per unit area. If we have a uniform intensity of magnetic lines in a region and introduce a magnetic iron bar, all lies of force in the surroundings will bend and try to get into the bar. In effect, the bar is concentrating the flux to achieve more intensity. That is why the cores of electromagnets are made of iron. Similarly, the electric fields have material properties that conduct more; this is called the dielectric constant of the material. More dielectric constants concentrate the electric field. When both magnetic and electric fields exhibit this property, it is not surprising that electromagnetic fields like radio waves also exhibit the same properties. In fact this phenomenon is observed when the cell phone connection gets lost when we are in a lift. The steel frame of the lift is a good conductor of the waves, so all waves go into the shell and do not come inside, thus "shielding" the inside from the waves. The formulae of magnetism and electricity are remarkably similar. These concepts are also explained to children by comparing it to the flow of water in a tube. Here we see another example of the Law of Correspondence.

You might be wondering why I am indulging in this scientific diversion. My point is that, according to the Law of Correspondence, cosmic energy also follows the same principle. If we want more energy to flow through us, we need to offer the least path of resistance to it. How do we reduce the resistance? Resistance is caused by obstacles. Mind you, obstacles are not bad; in fact, we want them there in many cases. I will come to this point later. For now, let's say that, in order for water to flow freely through a long pipe, the pipe must be hollow and the sides must be smooth so as not to cause any friction to the flow of water current. The internal resistance in a copper wire is very low. This means large currents can flow through it; its conductivity is better than, say, rubber, wood, or iron. One point to note is that, if the energy inflow is equal to the outflow, then the wire itself gets nothing even if large currents pass through it. If there is a circuit that does something, for example, a TV or a motor, then that circuit offers resistance to the flow of current, but the energy transfer is a desired output, hence my point in saying that all obstacles are not bad; they can be there by design. The point is that large currents do not flow through it as compared to the flow through a pure conductor. When large quantities of energy must be transmitted from a power station to a house, a very good conducting material is used. Even though large quantities of energy flow through it, the wire itself gets nothing and remains cool. If any resistance develops, for example, a loose joint, the wire will burn out in no time. When large amounts of energy are flowing, we have to be extremely careful.

Similarly, cosmic energy in large quantities can be channelled by people who have very little internal resistance. These are people who have very few obstacles to the energy flow in them. If such a person exists, all energy that would have otherwise been spread out goes through him or her, creating a high intensity of energy. This is similar to the power cable. People would like to go to the power cable to get some energy for themselves. If this is attempted by those who have some desires, due to the large energy flow, they will either be heated or destroyed immediately. Others going to these people will receive energy exactly relative to the amount they are wired up for.

Similarly, there are people who can conduct large quantities of energy and transmit it to others. Our own parents, by their attention, transfer energy to us. Most of us derive our energies from parents when we are infants. Slowly the kids find other sources of energies – maybe teachers or other kids by their encouragement and support. I want to point out the importance of gurus, no matter the level of their proficiency. Our gurus may be great or may not be that great. They themselves may be on the path of realization with a limited amount of energy, which is more than what we have but not as much, maybe, as a great guru. There is a tendency amongst people to be disillusioned by one guru and hope to go to a higher guru. What we need to be careful of here is that we also have a capacity to absorb and spend energy. People sometime say that one guru is not as great as another guru, and hence they want to change gurus. What is to be realized is that we are looking at the energy flow into us. Granted our guru may not be as great as another guru, which our own guru also acknowledges. However, we have to see what is suitable to us based on our capacity. It is like a small bulb saying that it will not bother to connect to a battery cell; rather, it will go to the highest source of energy, which is a power cord in the house. It will be burnt out in milliseconds. Finally, the energy is same in both and the energy just trickles down to various levels. We should be grateful that energy sources that are suitable to us are made available. The battery itself may be charged by the power cord via a charger, but that is totally irrelevant to us. The bulb should go to the battery for energy; similarly, we should go to a guru who is suited to our capacity. Later we will see that, when the disciple is ready, the guru appears.

Magnetism and Magnetic Personalities

We could take a small detour here while we are discussing Ohm's law and current. We know that current is a movement of charge, and that, itself, produces a magnetic field. That is why, wherever there are large currents, we observe magnetic effects around it. If the current is made to go around a coil, we get an even more focused magnetic field. Induction furnaces act on this principle. A varying magnetic field is applied to iron pieces. These induce oscillations in the iron pieces, and since they have resistance, they heat up and melt. Similarly, in a microwave oven, food is heated by induction. The equivalent of that should be that high energies flowing through us would produce high influential fields, which could influence others who come near it. That is the origin of the term "magnetic personality". Now, the larger the energy flowing in them, either due to low internal resistance or by higher voltages in them, the more pronounced is the field around them.

These fields themselves have a particular frequency. For example, an alternating current (AC) through a wire would produce an AC magnetic field around it, and a radio frequency current would transmit radio waves around it. Even people have particular frequencies with which they affect others. So highly positive people influence others around them by their very presence. We are all aware of highly negative people who can achieve nothing themselves and make sure others don't either. So, if you want to be successful, surround yourself with highly positive people who themselves have achieved something – anything for that matter. Their fields will induce you to also be successful.

Also, when a current-carrying conductor comes across a magnetic field, it experiences a force. So if energy is flowing through us and we go near a person who is also creating a field, we experience a force either towards or away from it. Thus we find that, for no apparent reason, we are attracted to some people while we cannot bear to be near others. The only way we can be near a field and yet not experience a force is when we ourselves do not to carry a current; in other words, we have no reaction to the others' fields. If two current-carrying conductors with high currents are brought close together, it is not possible for them not to exert a mutually equal force. Either they are attracted strongly or are repelled. Hence, if you are strongly attracted or repelled by a person, you should know your options. Either you should continue your state of thinking and thereby your field, or, if you don't want to be influenced, just reduce your own flow for some time. For example, if a person is angry and is inducing anger in you too, you could either continue so as to make him or her really wild, or just stop reacting to dissipate some of the energy. Of course another option is to try and induce an opposite effect on the angry person by sending out calm thoughts. The success of this strategy depends on how much you can influence the other person without becoming influenced yourself.

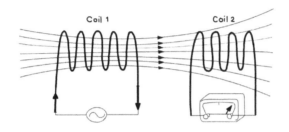

The topics we think are the energy fields we radiate. If we think money all the time, the energy attracts similar topics, people and circumstances. How powerful the attraction is depends on how much the energy field we create which is proportional to the energy flow within us.

In short, every person radiates a field of energy when large amounts of energy are flowing in him or her. Large amounts of energy flow if a person feels strongly about something. If a person is generally pure (low internal resistance), the energy flow is higher, and hence the field strength is greater. When many individuals who radiate similar energy get together, the energy is increased, and the fields get stronger. Every field affects other energy-producing bodies. The reactions are definite and quantifiable. We can try to produce the energy field we want to have; we can increase our success by surrounding ourselves with people who have similar energies. Light is energy, but when all waves that make it act in phase, we get LASER.

That is why *satsang* (literally means association with good people), or being near a guru, is so important. Depending upon the power of the guru, he will influence his disciples when they are near him. The high energy flowing in the master induces energy in the disciples. The important point to note is that being induced by the guru when we are full of internal resistance will only heat us up and finally burn us out. Preparation from our side to receive the energy constructively is an absolute must.

All initiations are connections to high-energy sources. Examples are the *Gayathri mantra* (one of the sacred mantras) initiation, the Shaktipath initiation, the Reiki initiation, and I am sure these would be rituals in the church and in Buddhist temples. These can be done only by competent gurus. However, the caution remains the same: connecting to a higher source without decreasing internal resistance will only blow a few fuses. If high voltage is applied to a resistor that cannot handle it, it will be destroyed. Similarly, if we connect a small radio to a high-voltage AC mains in a house, it will blow out. In general, application of a high-voltage source burns up the smaller stuff. On the other hand, other circuits that could not function due to insufficient voltage would start working. For example a TV that was connected to a battery does not function but when the voltage increased when connected to the mains started functioning. Similarly, when we are initiated into any mantra – *Shaktipath* – the smaller stuff like small desires and petty quarrels burn up and hold no more interest. On the other hand, circuits that seem superhuman light up and cause, for example, an ability to foretell the future or see into the distance. However, when the currents become larger, even these may go away. If we get attached to any one particular circuit and its activities, due to the internal resistance, it will start heating us up. We will then have the choice of either living with this achievement by reducing the voltage, thereby making no more progress, or burning up this skill and going higher. In other words, don't get attached to the *siddhis* (paranormal powers); proceed for ultimate realization.

So the objective is to decrease our internal resistance and connect to a high potential source for meditation.

What Is It That We Are Really After? How Do We Get It? Mantra Chanting

As I explained in the previous section, what we are really after is the large rush, or flow, of energy. The energy flow can be increased either by storing up energy, by reducing internal resistance to the flow, or by both.

Methods for reducing internal resistance are explained, in general and in very great detail, in almost all religious books. All religions, in some way, prescribes elaborate dos and don'ts, and this list should be updated with the times. Internet addiction and social media need to be added! In simple terms, the aim is to keep thoughts absolutely at a minimum with no attachments.

However, I now want to talk about another topic regarding the storing up of energy. Remember, energy in this context is defined as the attention the higher level gives to the lower-level entity. For example, the attention we give a particular thought is energy to that thought. If we need energy, we need to attract the attention of the higher-level source.

If our thought makes us happy, we give the poor chap a benevolent look; if the thought makes us angry or disgusted, we try to kill it off somehow. Thus the thought, by the behaviour it induces in us, makes us give it a particular energy. As far as the thought is concerned, if it behaves in a particular way, it gets good things; otherwise, it is killed. It sees a "different god" for different invocations.

Chanting mantras is one way of building up energy. Mantras have the capability of invoking a reaction in the higher planes. The higher plane then gives us attention and wants us to continue further. The higher plane removes all obstacles we face if we are pleasing it. In spite of any turmoil, we are miraculously rescued, and we are protected as long as we continue to do what the higher level wants us to. Does this sound like a god to you? We do the same thing to our thoughts. God does the same to us.

If we continuously chant our chosen mantra, two things happen simultaneously. First, we don't think other thoughts, thereby reducing the internal resistance I was talking about. Second, we build up more energy of the kind we want.

If things were so simple, why does everyone who prays not get a vision – an opportunity to see – his or her lord? Why are they not becoming so powerful that they achieve what they want? Is this really a foolproof method?

The answer to this lies in the fact that, after the buildup of even a little energy, we have countless ways of discharging it. A fool and his money are easily parted! Because we build up some energy as we chant, the things we do after that are fuelled by more energy and are therefore more enjoyable. We immediately end up discharging that energy. In some cases this may be a good thing. Remember, all of us have some capacity for storing up energy. A small capacitor may store a small amount of energy, and if it is forced to store additional energy, it may just burst. More likely it will find a path of discharge that will be very pleasurable, but sometimes totally useless.

In my view, it is easiest to build up energy by chanting a mantra. A few minutes or an hour of chanting is not the problem. The hours we spend after that is the problem. Many people switch on the TV after *pooja* (reverence or worship), or read mail after meditation. This discharges all the good work done. And we wonder why our meditations are not of any use.

Even if we are careful in the next few hours after the mantra chanting, there are a lot of hidden devils in the mind. All those thoughts that wanted more energy now have it made! Your every glance at the thoughts gives them much more energy than you gave them before. If previously you had to spend an hour to give a thought some energy, now a mere flash in time will activate it. Thus, things become more powerful after meditation. Anger comes easily, as it is also a form of energy. If previously you were too tired to be angry, now you have all the energy in the world! So are lustful thoughts illumined by the newfound energy. Thus, when you chant mantras, the risks of negative results are increased. As you get more rigorous in your mantra chanting, the risk of falling down becomes more severe! Previously you had a little money, and small-time beggars were after you. Now you have more money, and dacoits (armed robbers!) are after you! Stones are thrown only at fruit bearing trees! Is this the result of mantra chanting and meditation? Then we should stop it! That is why mantra chanting by itself will not work unless we also clear our minds of all negativities. And that is where the hard work is. The negative thoughts are like furniture or decorative objects that we brought into the house. Each piece looked good at that time, but now there is no space. There is no room for new things to come inside, in addition we must continue to maintain all of them. The only way is to throw some of them out, but we don't want to admit that we made a mistake buying the pieces, or we give an excuse for buying it.

Remember, I said that even though a conductor transfers a really high-energy flow, the conductor itself takes nothing. It offers no resistance. It has no circuits it wants activated from the flow of current. If it attempted any such thing it would burn out immediately.

Thus, mantra chanting is a must, but it has to be accompanied by cleaning up the mind (*Chitta Suddhi*).

How to Meditate

Whatever method you choose, remember that the whole point of meditating is to think deeply about – nothing. The purpose is to build up energy. A necessary step to that was to reduce the number of thoughts, otherwise the energy will get discharged. We will be in continuous ecstasy commensurate with the level of energy we build up.

As we saw in the previous section, we need to increase the current flow significantly. This is possible either by decreasing the internal resistance, by increasing the voltage, or by both. Of course large amounts of current causes heating, so the increase must be done in a gradual manner; otherwise, we will burn out. The heating is dependent on the flow of current (actually the square of the current) and the internal resistance. No heating happens when the resistance is zero.

All meditation techniques attempt one of the two things: to decrease the internal resistance and to connect to a higher source. The first one is totally up to the person, and the second is totally up to the guru. Of course, both are necessary if we are to achieve a decent amount of energy flow.

Internal resistance, as we saw, is wholly dependent upon thoughts. Now, these thoughts are actually structured, and these structured thoughts pose more resistance than the loose thoughts. The structured thoughts are like circuits in electricity. For example, if a circuit is nothing but a combination of wires and resistances, coils, and the like, which acts like a bulb, we will have light when energy flows through it. If the circuit happens to be a circuit like a TV, we get to see great videos on it. The structured thoughts are what we ourselves created or are in the process of creating. For example, if we are practicing music, we build a set of thoughts. We build some memories of tunes, some knowledge of rules and ideas, and activate this thought structure. For others it could be painting. We, of course, have many structures within us, which we ourselves have forgotten or unaware. When energy flows, the phenomenon it was built for manifests. Various circuits need various power levels. A small bulb requires a small battery, while a TV or a water heater would not run on the same battery. Similarly, a high-energy source, if connected to a small bulb, would simply blow the bulb away.

We are all endowed with a small source of energy connection; that is how we are alive. There are circuits in the body and mind that consume this energy. We saw in previous sections that, when the energy taken into the circuit and that which is expended are almost the same, we maintain equilibrium. It is possible to take in more energy than we spend, and thereby start building up energy within us. This extra energy could be used to switch on other circuits that could not be activated with a smaller source. These are what we see as *Kriyas*, or manifestations of creative thoughts and deeds.

The summary of these ideas is that, even with our existing source of energy, it is possible to store up energy by cleaning up the mental plane. This is what we call Chitta Suddhi.

Chitta Sudhi can be done in many ways. Here are five suggestions:

1) Consider a garden. It has many small and lovely plants as well as forest-like growth. There are animals, birds and insects feeding. You want to clear the garden. The first step is to isolate the garden and prevent sunlight from entering. The plants will die. Soon the vegetarian insects will die, and then the carnivorous beings will also die. In a similar way, if we liken our mental plane to a jungle, we can liken the sunlight to our attention – our awareness – of the jungle. If we simply don't allow any attention into this thought complex, the whole thing will be cleared soon. However, this is easier said than done. Mainly it is because we are partial to some plants (after all we planted them) like the flowers or the vegetables. If we are not attached to anything, clearing the garden is very easy. Even if we decide we are not attached to any one thing in the garden, the sunlight is continuously falling, and we need to divert it somewhere. Hence the technique of mantra chanting. By continuously chanting the mantra, our attention is diverted, and the mental forest is cleared away due to lack of attention, which, as we know, is energy. However, this technique will kill everything, both that which you desire to be there and that which you want to kill

(both the desired plants and the weeds). If we can selectively focus the light on the plants that we want to grow, then we will kill the remaining vegetation.

2) Our mental plane is like the real world. Everyone (every thought in the mental plane) wants to get energy by hook or crook. Some get it directly from the source, like plants in the real world and sattvic (pure) thoughts in the mental plane. As most of the thoughts come up for our attention, we are caught up with that train of thought and we are engaged, thereby giving that thought complex the energy it needs. But the other thoughts are not fools. They wait for the slightest opportunity and jump in, claiming to be an enticing point you should consider. That is why, when we are thinking about a particular topic, after some time, another thought with no connection of logic or time or anything comes up. We briefly decide which thought train to follow, the first one or the second. The process continues on and on. The thoughts that receive energy go back refreshed and come up again when the conditions are ripe. Now the second thought should be of an energy level almost equal to the first; otherwise it would not have been able to dislodge the first. That is the connection actually. The second thought is of the same intensity as the first. That is also the reason that, when we are worrying about something, we need some thought equally powerful to dislodge it. As it turns out, this is often another worry!

Now consider this situation: When thoughts come up for our attention, we look at them but refuse to follow them. Let the first thought come and do its song and dance. However enticing it may be, we don't give it energy. Instead, we let it spend energy trying to impress us. The thought suddenly realizes that it is not getting the energy it had hoped for. It slinks away hoping to catch us later. Now perhaps another thought, which previously did not have as much energy as the first but now has become an equal, will come to the arena. It will try its luck. If you also refuse to follow this thought, it too goes away. In this manner, in the decreasing order of energy intensity of the thoughts, they die or they are weakened, and they withdraw to catch you at a more opportune time. This was what I referred to as "excretion of undigested thoughts" in the previous section. This is also roughly the theory of Transcendental Meditation. Just observe your thoughts.

3) *Bhakti yoga* (devotion to a chosen god) and *karma yoga* (to do our duty with the intention of getting purified) act as great enhancers for Chitta Sudhi. If we don't care about the result, will we entertain any thoughts or worries? If we believe we are God's agent, will we bother to worry? These two practices also clear the mind and our internal resistance of the mind.

4) Of course, we could understand the whole principle and understand the need for Chitta Sudhi and consciously clear the mental jungle. Once we understand the need and we also understand the games of the mind, we will clear it easily. We don't need a rulebook; we just *know* what to do. This is roughly *gnana yoga*. We realize the theory of this, and we see the tricks of the thoughts. The thoughts just burn under our intense scrutiny.

5) There is another method, known as Shaktipath. Shaktipath is one person conferring psychic energy upon another. This method is to set fire to the forest; in other words, to introduce intense energy to the forest. If the wood is dry, like dry thoughts, they are burnt easily. If the wood is wet or thick it may not catch fire. However, this energy makes no distinction. It burns all. So, if we have any attachment, we would not know if this is good or bad. Also, if we are growing more thoughts than are being burnt, this method will not show progress. However, if we build up a good fire, nothing can stop it – whether the wood is dry or wet.

The summary of these methods is that we need Chitta Sudhi; otherwise, we will not have a good energy flow. It is also required for the second method, where the guru connects us to a higher source.

In all initiations, like Shaktipath initiation or Gayathri initiation, the connection is raised to a higher potential. Now, this by itself may not yield much. Thought voltage is high. If the resistance is equally higher, very little energy flows. Yes, it is more than what was normally flowing, but both are not significant. The real benefits start to show up only when the internal resistance is reduced; in other words, Chitta Sudhi is achieved. Thus, no point blaming a guru or a system if you yourself have much work to do!

So how do we meditate? Chose any method for Chitta Sudhi. If you work with a guru who can connect you to a higher source, consider yourself lucky. As and when the energy levels flowing through you increase, more circuits will get switched on. Enjoy the effects!

There will come a stage when the energy flow gets to high levels. That is when you get to a state of superconductivity, or continuous energy flow with no input. In other words, *Sachidananda* (ever in a state of bliss). This creates the stage for the next step - enlightenment.

The Law Applied to Moksha, or Enlightenment

At the outset, I have to admit that I must humbly submit my thoughts on this topic on which spiritual giants have spoken. There is also the question any reader would ask – if I really knew how to attain nirvana, why am I hanging around here? However, as I mentioned in the introduction, I am discussing the thought process of applying the Law of Correspondence to this subtle topic, and hopefully something good may come of it. If it makes sense to even one reader, the effort will have been worthwhile.

This discussion is a tough one, and many texts – sacred texts, stories, lectures, and poems – over the centuries have tried to explain this concept. Apparently, this is so simple that we miss it! That is because the topic is not about the object; rather, it is about the very subject "I". My attempt is to crack open the case using the Law of Correspondence.

What Is Moksha?

In general, Moksha is understood to be deliverance from this cycle of birth and death. Of course we cannot answer this question in detail because, if we attain moksha, we have gone to another level and then we could never think of coming back to the lower level. Even if that person came back, we would not understand what that person is trying to say.

That is because there is no vocabulary in this world to describe the other. To solve the problem, we can make use of the Law of Correspondence.

The equivalent question in the dream world would be, does any thought in the dream state benefit by the dreamer waking up? If it does, what is the process by which it can wake up?

We of course know that it is not possible for any one thought to wake up while others are sleeping. It is possible for the "I" observer in the dream to wake up and thereby wake up all thoughts. This leads to the more serious question as to who this "I" is. The "I" is a commonality in all states, so it is the only "real" thing. The "I" in the dream and the "I" in the waking state are the same. Else it is not possible for the same person to say; this was my dream and this is my reality. So by the Law of Correspondence, the same "I" would be there when we are emancipated and become the god of our current world.

The main question is, can a single thought awaken us to a higher reality. We said this was not possible without waking the whole dreamer. In fact, when the "I" dreamer wakes up, all thoughts are seen as nothing but an illusion created in the person himself or herself. What is possible is that one thought can wake up the dreamer either by being very painful or by becoming full of energy in some way.

I wish there was a laid-out method, a set of steps to be followed for one who meditates to attain *moksha*.

This is similar to the dreamer realizing his or her true self by waking up. But is there a method to wake up from your dream? The questions to ask before that are: Why did we sleep in the first place? What did we want to achieve when we fell asleep? Is it not true that we ourselves wanted to rest a bit and create the dreams for our own entertainment? The problem is that we forgot about that when we fell asleep. How did we fall asleep?

Let us look at ways we wake up, because we are already in a dream and we have to wake up from the dream. Ideally the waking up has to be done in a premeditated way; for example, while in the waking state, we set an alarm. This also leads to the route of preordained fate and leaving things to fate. A time-bound yuga (an epoch or era within a four-part cycle), as mentioned before, could be caused by this. Maybe the world will suddenly stop after a time.

But once in the dream, there are a few ways for the dreamer to wake up:

1. Concentrate on why you are dreaming this dream. What problem needs to be solved? What was the intention of getting into this dream? What is the theme of the dream? For example, the theme might be to enjoy something, to analyze something, or to finish some work.

2. Raise hell in the dream literally, and make things too much to bear. You must take note and wake up.

3. Simply stop all dreaming activities. Everything becomes a blank. In the blankness you may suddenly realize that you exist in a way you were not aware of before.

4. Recognize that you can never wake up by yourself but can only request in a humble manner to the higher "I" and wait as long as it takes.

5. Observe all that you are dreaming. Suppose you are dreaming that you are a king. Observe that you are observing that you are a king. Know that you can also observe nothing so logically; you must be the witness to many births. This is only logical thinking. By constantly thinking about this, in a flash you may awaken, and then it all will make sense. Till then, it is all nonsense and very difficult to explain to others, even to other fellow characters in the dream.

None of this will, of course, guarantee that you will wake up. These are all different paths people sometimes follow. Setting an alarm is like God himself waking you up; no action is required of you. The first one is self-discovery – a "who am I?" type of thinking. The second one is severe penance, tapas, or being followed by the demons in our mythology. The third one is meditation by slowly reducing your thoughts to a few and possibly to only one thought, and then to none, the classical mediation technique. The fourth one is the *Bhakti marga* – you just surrender and wait. As I said before, waking up happens in a flash, and you wake up when the right conditions are met. The last one is gnana yoga or the path of knowledge.

What Is Enlightenment?

When we wake up, you suddenly realise that you were dreaming and all the characters and objects in the dream are yourself. In short, you realised your god like status with respect to the dream. This is enlightenment, realising that you are the god of the current world we live in.

It is important to note that, when we wake up, the dream state in its entirety is dissolved. The problem comes when we want some things in the dream to end but we want some to continue.

Of what use is it for a thought to wake up? In the short duration when the dreamer is awake, it is possible to look down and decide if things are going well or not, and by a mere wish, change the entire situation of the dream. In that sense, the enlightenment of that thought or character has benefited the situation. That is true, however, only if the ego reverts back to the dream state; otherwise, the entire dream state stands dissolved.

How Do We Achieve It?

So what is the guaranteed method of attaining Moksha and Enlightenment? Observe the brief period when you wake up. Let us not take the examples of violent dreams for the moment, as they tend to be exceptions. You are observing your thoughts. Your number of thoughts has decreased in intensity. You are suddenly "aware" that you are thinking or seeing your thoughts. This is the most crucial moment in waking up. Since there is a vacuum of thoughts, you could fill the space with more dream thoughts, or let the vacuum remain and just observe yourself, noticing that you are observing. Suddenly you wake up to realize that you were actually dreaming and you were actually dreaming another world. These are critical moments. If you decide to dream more dream thoughts, you go back to sleep. If you decide to pursue the thoughts, you need to do so when you wake up. Now you have attained "moksha" from the dreamer's point of view.

In that short duration in which the higher self is looking at the lower self, there is nothing that is impossible to be achieved at the lower level. Once awake, we can rewrite the dream the way we want it to be.

Going further, by the Law of Correspondence, while we are all powerful after waking up from the dream world, we might not feel great because the higher level has its own set of problems. Maybe we are relieved that it was all only a dream. Indeed, is there an end to the number of times we must wake up to a higher reality? If the happiness is unchanged by waking by one level, would it be any better if we jumped a thousand levels? Where is the end to waking up to a higher level?

There is a theory about the discrete state of electrons about their orbits. They are either at one level or the next level. These levels are well defined and are called orbitals. By excitement (the addition of energy) they can rise to a higher-level orbit, and when they come back down one level, they release energy. This energy is also very precise and comes out only in the form of a particular frequency. Thus, the stars or a sodium vapour lamp exhibit a particular frequency of light when they are excited and then come back to their original levels.

I would say this similar to the case of awareness. Either it will be at my dream level, or my waking level. Similarly, the awareness will be at my cellular level, or my current level, or what I call God level. Not in between. To raise the awareness from one level to the other, energy is required or released.

So, once again, what is a failsafe method of attaining moksha? Do not identify with the current-state thoughts. Observe the "I" which is the observer, and suddenly you realize a higher "I". Simple, isn't it?

We do it every day when we wake up from our dreams!

Methodology of Shaktipath, Kundalini Yoga, and Similar Traditions

Shaktipath neatly combines both methods – Chitta Sudhi and the connection to a higher source. When a connection to a higher source happens, an increase of energy flow occurs. How much higher depends totally upon the internal resistance (Chitta Sudhi in other words). Students who are alert and notice the change automatically de-focus on the mental forest. This decreases the forest growth as mentioned in the previous sections. This increases the energy flow.

We have learned that this increase in the energy flow switches on other circuits. In other words, Kriyas manifests. This is a great source of marvel to students initially, something which they never knew existed within them. Actually what has happened is that the thought structure (mental circuits) existed before, either partially mastered during this birth or from previous births. If the energy levels were sufficient, they would have already manifested themselves and there would be no wonder in their occurrence. We would have attributed this to being "born gifted". However, additional energy required to switch on a circuit would be possible only by the combination of a connection to a higher source and Chitta Sudhi. When the circuit gets switched on, we get a Kriya. We hear of Sadhaks, people who suddenly sing, compose poetry, paint, and the like. This is caused by the increased energy they experienced. One thing to note is that, if the energy levels increase, one circuit may get burnt out even as others are getting switched on. For example, a small bulb may start glowing initially, but as we increase the voltage, it may blow up while a TV continues to work just fine. So the Kriyas manifest for some time and then go away while others manifest. The sad or good part of the whole thing is that the ultimate goal of the energy flowing within us (the shakti) is to burn all circuits and give us the path of no resistance for so that we are joyful forever. Once we allow the forest fire to build up (Kundalini shakti) there will be no stopping it.

All of us have some energy flowing through us; otherwise we would not be alive. As we saw in previous sections, how much energy flows through us depends entirely on how much resistance we offer to the flow of energy. The energy is impeded by our thoughts and actions. When the energy flows, if we hinder it by asking it to do some work – for example, thinking about something – then the energy does that work, but at an increased resistance level. More energy flowing in the same path in general increases heat and, eventually, burnout. Thus repeated thinking on the same topic can burn us out, as can be seen when we worry excessively. If, in our conscious state, we take care not to think any thoughts by sort of emptying the mind, great energy flow occurs in our minds and bodies. But this could be dangerous. If this extra energy is used to continue our worrying, more heating will occur! Hence we should be careful in handling this extra energy. If we leave the energy to flow wherever it wants, it will go to the desires that are prevalent at the time and burn them up if we do not interfere in any way. This builds momentum, and pretty soon this becomes a strong force that can be used by the *sadhak* (one who has yet to reach a goal) to make his channel pure and offer least resistance to the flow. In the process, the energy flow produces a field around it that will gather similar people, thoughts, and energies. Thus gurus and *sishyas* (disciples) will come together at the right times and exchange energies. In this whole process there are multiple and varied energy channels. Some carry such high energies that it is impossible for us to approach them (think of high-tension power cables). Some are transformers in the sense that they can access the high-energy source and convert it to something we can absorb. We should not undermine their importance. Thus, even though our own guru may not be that much of an ideal, he is still the one who connects us to the source; hence we need to respect him. We should not think that we should connect only to greatest guru and disregard all the others. We may burn out if we get near a guru not meant for us. We ourselves should not hesitate to pass on energy to people who need a still-lower form of energy. For parents it is mandatory to pass on energy to their kids. Thus we have a dharma (a duty, a principle of cosmic order) to pass on energy to those who need it; that is how the universe runs. From an individual standpoint, more energy flows increase our joy, and that is what we are all after.

Renunciation

Almost all religious books and teachings advocate renunciation – giving up – and that is a great source of pain to most of us. Almost every teaching says that, unless we let go, we will not soar. In the previous section we saw that we need to reduce the number of our thoughts. The only way to do this is to renounce any attachment to our thoughts. But according to the Law of Correspondence, we need to practice renunciation in the real world if we are to be successful in renouncing our attachment to our thoughts.

However, for the most part, we are unwilling to let go of anything that is ours. This refers not only to physical possessions, but also to our ideas and beliefs. We do not want to discuss our ideas and beliefs lest someone proves them wrong and we have to give them up. At the energy level, it is understandable. We have stored a lot of energy in these things, and energy is what we are all after, so these things are storehouses of our energy, which we draw for our enjoyment later. We get angry if the energy is being taken away. But the truth is that there is only so much energy we can store, and even that is stored in an inefficient way. When we have an electric socket, who needs a battery? Those connected to the source can renounce all energy storehouses.

But this is very difficult as can be seen even in advanced sages, as in the case of Jaigishavya, Warrior of Light. I am again referring to Pandit Rajmani Tigunait's book, *From death to Birth: Understanding Karma and Reincarnation page 27*. Jaigishavya, after intense austere practices, penetrated the higher levels of consciousness and was in *Samadhi* (a trance state of meditative consciousness). He was presented his *sanchita* karmas. (Sanchita karmas are karmas that are you accumulated from all your births; *prarabda* karma is just for this birth.) He saw all the previous lives he had lived – king, beggar, lion, scorpion, and the like. These extended as far as he could see into the horizon, and there seemed to be more beyond what he could see. In all of this, he had taken each of these forms to fulfil something he wanted to experience only to realize that he wanted more; hence, he was reborn as another species. Yet he still had some unfulfilled desires. So far, he had enthusiasm for penance and samadhi, but seeing this, Jaigishavya gave up. It was not possible to come out of this cycle. He could not even finish fully even one birth, let alone the million births he had taken. It was then that as an agent of Vishnu, sage Avatya, came to him to guide him. Jaigishavya had gone as far as an individual can go with self-effort. After this, no human teacher or scriptures can guide. Sage Avatya asked some simple questions and finally said, "Why are you worried about the unfulfilled desires in each one of the births? They don't need to be fulfilled. It is just that you are attached to each and still want to live it to the fullest and finish any unfinished business. Just drop the entire set and come with me." So saying, Sage Avatya guided him, advising him to drop all attachments to the fruits of karmas. This renunciation will work as passive help for most thoughts that are weak. For stronger karmas, he advised a systematic practice, which when worked in spite of all difficulties will finally redeem you. Soon Jaigishavya became attained moksha.

I introduced this tale to illustrate this point: As in small things, so in big things, as in big things, so in small things. If we are not able to give up small things, we will never be able to give up an entire birth out of a million births. Jaigishavya wanted to finish each and every birth. Each and every birth had minor unfinished business. If these minor issues had not been left behind at the end of each birth, he would not have seen the millions of unfulfilled births. So the path is to renounce the fruits of actions in the small things, and the big things will take care of themselves, or can be achieved easily. However all this is easy to say. If an accomplished person like Jaigishavya experienced confusion over this, what about ordinary mortals like us? We cannot even delete some photos we have from our hard disks! Is it even worth attempting?

Some of us may mock Jaigishavya and say we are not like that. When we reach that high state, we think, we will have no hesitation in giving up. But consider our state today. We in a rare moment of clarity, and we see our thoughts laid before us. This is rare and sometimes comes when we stop thinking any new thoughts, like during meditation. We see thoughts in various themes – "office thoughts", "family thoughts", "sports thoughts", and so forth. All these correspond to the various avatars we adopt in life. In each one of them we have unfinished business. We came out of that thought primarily because we diverted our energy to another thought and pulled it out of the first thought. We could, of course, go back to any one thought and revive it. All these residual thoughts still have some energy left and are waiting for our one glance to start dancing again. Do we not feel tired and dejected seeing the enormity of the task in front of us? We don't want to drop any thought; all seem equally important. Even if we want to drop one, that thought will not leave us. It is energized by our very thought of abandoning it! Our situation is in no way different than Jaigishaivya's situation. What is the way out? Someone has to come to us at this stage and tell us that all this is a dream, and none of it matters. We must wake up and drop all of this in one go. Easier said than done?

Fortunately for us, there are many scriptures that advise us not to be worried about the enormity of the task, but to just begin. Even if we die when we are only halfway finished, Krishna, in the Bhagavad Gita, has promised that we can either continue from where we left off, or be born into a rich family to enjoy life while we take a breather.

How do we apply the Hermetic law here? As in small things, so in big things. As in our mind, so in our dreams, and so in our various births.

So let us start by renouncing the small things – a few knickknacks lying around the house, a little time to help others, some donations to charities that will not hurt our financial situation, some preconceived notions, and so forth. The mechanism of giving up a small thing or a big thing is the same. We can start by staying away from it, by not actively pursuing it, by understanding why we are doing it, and so forth. Better still is not to expect any outcome; then we would never be attached at all. When we renounce a small thing, we drop the associated things that cling to it. This mass has been sticking to other things and soon it turned into a big mess. Dropping small things automatically prevents big things from building up. If you are not attached to your ego, nothing builds up!

Applying All of This Theory

Let us get back to what all of us want. I have explained these concepts in various sections. In this section, I will tie it all together.

No matter whom we ask, it is clear that everyone wants joy and happiness. The methods of deriving joy may be different, the objects they think will give them joy are different, but we are all after the same unadulterated joy. And, of course, we want it forever, not for a fleeting moment.

We have also discovered that, loosely, the joy we get is directly proportional to the amount of flow of energy we experience, like a heavy flow of water or electric current. Now we also have seen that our minds have internal resistances in the form of "circuits" that dissipate power. So, any flow of energy will be dampened. How quickly this happens depends on the amount of resistance. In addition, a large flow of current under resistance will produce heat, so overly strong emotions in a thought-filled mind will create enormous stress.

Now great joy – meaning a large flow of energy – can occur when we have high pressure (voltage), or low pressure paired with low resistance. An example of high pressure would be a bolt of lightning. An example of low pressure and low resistance would be a large river flowing gently without any obstructions.

The first method for deriving joy is to increase the pressure by intense thought and by some chants. The second method is to rid your mind of all desires and let the energy flow. We have problems with both the methods. It is not possible to increase the pressure to such levels; if we were to do so, the energy burns up everything. In the second method, we cannot reduce desires to low enough values to provide us with any benefit.

The only method we know and apply consistently is to build a container (a capacitor in electrical terms) and pump energy into it. At an appropriate time, a trigger built into the container releases the energy. Or, at a high pressure, the energy bursts out on its own. Let me give an example. We believe that, if a certain thing happens or we acquire a certain thing, we will experience supreme bliss. Perhaps there is a small amount of truth to this idea. We might want a good meal in a restaurant, or we might want a certain person to behave in a desired way, or we might want a racing car! The objects of our desire (the containers) are different, but we are all building containers, whether they are people, things, pets, events, or even ideas. We build so much energy into a container, and if somebody steals it from us, or attempts to do so, or hints that there is no joy in it, we get very angry.

Some containers are small and flexible; for example, a joke. It builds up mildly, and then we experience a sudden release of energy (a small amount of energy in a short time), which is still a large current momentarily. It gives us a sudden burst of joy, and we laugh. Of course, this joke should not affect in any way the other containers we have been building. Some containers are steel containers that can withstand high pressures and large amounts of energy. A musician might describe bliss as a particular combination of notes. A racing enthusiast might describe bliss as driving a Formula One car. Each would be right from his or her own standpoint. Each could develop a large flow of energy through his or her respective container.

The problem with the container approach is that we always mistake the container for the joy. An empty container would give us no joy. We actually must build up the pressure. Good Italian food is a container. It may evoke no reaction initially. Later, we make enquiries and find there is a popular Italian restaurant nearby. Of course, but it is always busy, your friend tells you. You need advance booking. Your attention level goes up, and you start pumping in energy into the container. What is so good about the restaurant? Well they make their own cheeses in Italy and import them. Vegetables are organically grown. More energy gets pumped into the container. The cheese just melts in your mouth, someone says. Now the energy in the container is reaching its peak. You secure a reservation. The moment the first bite enters your mouth, the container releases all the energy, and you get bliss for a second. If you don't get the reservation, the container bursts and heats up your brain, which we see as anger. Perhaps your dining partner has not experienced the anticipation and therefore the buildup of pressure that you have. You ask, "How is it?" The response is merely, "OK."

I leave it to you to come up with more examples. Our only mechanism of joy seems to be this: Select a container, build up the pressure in the container, and enjoy the fleeting rush of energy when it is released.

Is this the fate of humankind? Building containers for fleeting moments of joy? Is there no better method? Is it not possible to have joy forever?

One thing is clear, if we ask people to stop falsely identifying the container for the joy, they will revolt. "Are you stopping me from the only method I know?" they will ask. Or worse still, "I know there is joy in this. You also come and experience it."

We come back to the original question: How do we obtain unadulterated joy forever?

Not by the container approach, but the method requires practice.

Let me give an example. Once I was alone when my wife went away to visit her parents. She was pregnant at the time. I had a lot of time on my hands, so I decided to take up an accountancy course. The workload in the office was also light then. My formula for success was simple – no TV, no distractions, spend most of the time either studying or sleeping. Of course, I had a maid and a driver to look after the house and see to my transportation needs. Since I had decided voluntarily that I would not think of anything else other than study and sleep, the number of thoughts in my mind was reduced. This went on for a few months, and any change was gradual and not noticeable. I cleared my exams with ease and then went out with my friends for a game of tennis. Now, I am a beginner-level tennis player and am usually happy if my serve just gets to the other side of the net. But after I had limited my attention for three months, my alertness improved drastically. I was seeing the ball clearly and anticipating where it would go right after the toss up of the serve. I was clearly aware of the subtle variations of my shoulders, arms, and wrists, and when the racquet would strike the ball. The result was that none of my friends could take even one of my serves; I was continuously serving aces. They knew I had been studying and had never practiced, so we did not know how my game had improved. Later, after my wife came back home, I went back to my usual routine. Again, the change was gradual, but eventually my awareness went down to my normal levels, as did my tennis game.

I will now give a practical way of achieving continuous joy (or nearly continuous joy). It may sound boring and like nothing new, but it is still worth pursuing.

First, you must realize that the container is not joy. This is very important and fundamental. If we are sure of this fact, other things will follow. To give examples, the girl is not the joy, the music is not the joy, the food is not the joy, the car is not the joy; in fact no "thing" – physical, mental, or emotional – is joy. They are only containers of joy.

If these are containers are not joy itself, when we look or think about an object, we will not any gain joy from it. An empty container has to be filled before we can enjoy anything from it.

The first step is to remember that the container is not what we have to go after. We don't pursue our thoughts on anything consciously. We look at anything and say, "This is only a container. No point going after it."

This is a dangerous phase. Here we are, with the only source of joy (however fleeting) taken away from us. All our lives we have been going after containers. The containers have provided conflicts, and we have had to split our priorities. If we are not pursuing anything, then what are we supposed to do? Whatever we do is not going to give us joy, the very thing we are after!

This is when we apply the Law of Correspondence. In this world, what are we supposed to do? No idea. OK, apply Law of Correspondence and look one level below. What do you want your cells to do? You want them to do their appointed jobs!

This is exactly what we should focus on – doing our appointed jobs, as parents, teachers, employees, citizens – in all our roles. Of course we should not worry about the results of the actions of these roles because these are all containers, and we are not looking at them for any joy. We have to fulfil these roles to the best of our ability. This is exactly what God expects us to do.

Now suppose my eyes are doing a great job. I start seeing vibrant colour patterns that give me great joy. I would seek out good visual experiences, take good care of my eyes, maybe eat a few carrots to give more energy to my eyes. In short, when my organs do a good job, I give them more attention (energy). It is a similar situation in the thought world.

If we are not going after the containers, our minds are much more efficient. If we do our appointed jobs well, we get good results, which in turn is noticed by the higher level. More energy and attention will come our way. This is the Law of Correspondence.

I am not finished yet. We have still not reached the everlasting joy stage yet!

Our minds have always been after containers, and this will continue out of habit. Our minds will also try to entangle us. Remember, thoughts are also living things and will try their best to get our attention. Now that we are not after the containers in a conscious way, thoughts will creep in when we are not alert, and we will entertain them without conscious knowledge. This habit has to be broken, and this is the second stage of our purification. How do we break our unconscious habits?

Here the methods are many, but all of them involve not entertaining any of these thoughts. One classical method is to chant a mantra. This automatically keeps us from entertaining the other thoughts. An added bonus is that these mantras themselves have power. Another method is to be aware of each and every thought we are thinking. In that intense awareness, all the thoughts slink away. They come only when we are not alert. Slowly but surely, the thoughts lose energy and die out. We are now at the stage where we are not pursuing anything, and there are no random thoughts disturbing the scene. But we are still not full of joy yet.

This is, again, a dangerous phase. Previously we had fleeting joys even if, during the rest of the time, we felt sorrowful. Now we don't have sorrows, but we don't have any major joys either. That is because we are not taking the container approach, and the energy now is in a state of potentiality – there is no flow yet. At this stage, seekers can go astray and not enjoy this dry situation. Another danger is that, because the mind is clear, it is possible to follow any pursuit, and it will succeed given the clarity of thought. But the thoughts will go back to their normal positions soon.

This is when we need to introduce joys through containers, but we must not become attached to the containers. Let's look at the joy of giving – the joy of helping someone without expecting anything in return, the joy of singing a good song in praise of God. All these are good qualities, and they are containers. But it is easier for us to detach ourselves from these than it is to detach ourselves from other containers. It is very difficult to get too attached to the joy we get when we give to charity, for example. But we have to be careful because that this too is a container, even if it is a light one. The energy flow, however, is huge. Previously, when we had many thoughts in our minds, had we given to a charity we would have felt some happiness, but nothing compared to the flow we would get at this stage. Small things give tremendous joy at this stage. And they last longer.

We are getting closer now. We are getting joy for longer periods of time. Still, we are not at the stage where we are getting it all the time, naturally, and without effort.

Now is the time to apply the Law of Correspondence to our dream and waking states. I am there in the waking state, and I as an observer exist in the dream state too. How do we know? Well, the fact that you are saying you dreamt something means you were there, right? Last week somebody asked, "Who was the last to leave the party?" You said, "I saw Charles leave last." But the fact that you saw Charles leave means you yourself were still there, right? So there is an "I" in the dream state (lower level than my waking state) and there is also an "I" in the waking state, by the Law of Correspondence, one level above me as well. And, as the dreamer "I" and the waking "I" are the same, this dream which I am now seeing is also seen by the same I from a higher level. When you keep thinking about this topic, in a flash you are awake to a higher reality.

This is nirvana, or moksha. Why did I not advocate this last step in the beginning? Unless the dreamer stops dreaming, he or she will not wake up. Please look at the previous section on correspondence of the dream world.

In summary, the steps are:

- Don't mistake the containers of joy as joy.

- Do your assigned duty to the best of your ability.

- Get rid of the past tendencies.

- Cultivate gentle habits like giving to charity and helping others.

- At this stage, ask "Who is this "I" the observer?" and, in a flash, you will wake up to a higher reality and there will be nothing which you cannot achieve in this level.

This is exactly what the scriptures say and prescribe.

Some Miscellaneous Topics

How the Universe Was Made

In Hinduism, the Vedas, a large body of knowledge texts, describe how the universe was made. It is said that all forms of life; the concept of time and space; all the stars, the planets, the universe; and all that we see today came about at the same time, all at once, from Vishnu. It was not like the Darwinian world in which there was a gradual evolution. Well, after the evolution occurred, adjustments were made by Brahma. Brahma first created the perfect beings, and naturally they were not very interested in procreation because they were so lost in the bliss of just being. Hence Brahma, in his various states, created various type of beings – in his sleep, in his waking state, in his anger, and so forth – and these gave rise to various life forms and also instilled in them hunger, thirst, and sexual urges to help the cycle to continue. The various animals are described as coming from different parts of his body and from different mental states that he was experiencing. Thankfully we don't see the frightful Rakshasas (man eaters) and other frightening characters mentioned. However, the point is that all things were made at once. Brahma only rearranged a few properties and gave boosts to certain tendencies in the beings. This is similar to a dream we think about. All characters come, and the scene is set at one go. Later the characters play their roles with the other characters. Nothing new as such is created; the entire dream was created at one go.

Let us draw the parallel to the dream state. The dreamer, "I", creates all the material, roles, people, and circumstances for my own enjoyment. I create them all at once. Then, upon my waking, they are all dissolved to another "I", which we have seen is a higher-order reality, but has another higher order reality above it. As I created my dream world for my enjoyment, the higher-order god must have created this universe as a dream. The god himself would be in another dream and so on.

Moksha then seems to be waking up to the fact that the common "I" is a witness to all, and all are dreams one within the other. That is the real reason that the Law of Correspondence exists. If one level makes a dream level beneath it, it would then be sowing the seed of further dream worlds within. Is that not correct? How many such dream worlds exist? Well, that would be impossible to ascertain. If we go look up into the branches of a tree, we see innumerable leaves. However, if we look in the reverse direction, we see that all leaves and branches belong to one trunk only.

Is It Right to Kill Others? Is It Ever Justifiable?

For this we need to look at ourselves and how we relate to our cells in our bodies. Do we want our cells to start killing each other? Do we want our blood cells to move all over the place and say, "Kill the nerve cells"? Well that would be cancer, would it not? Is it OK for the white blood cells to kill harmful bacteria? Absolutely. That is what their role is. The question is, who lays down the roles and decides which killing is justifiable and which is not? The main point is, which life form are we are talking about? If we define the life as, say, our body, killing is justifiable if it is to maintain the system's stability. Thus, if harmful bacterial cells with an aim to destabilize our system are being killed, we say it is OK for the white blood cells to kill. But there are many bacterial cells that stabilize our bodies. Those are not to be killed. Our own cells may turn hostile to the system; they should be killed. We require quite an elaborate set of rules in order to determine when killing is justified.

Consider the country as a life form; a set of living things that owe allegiance to a concept called the country could be called as a life form.

If there are elements that want to destabilize the country, internal or external, it is OK for them to be killed. This is as defined by the entity called "country", which is a life form in its own right. However the same thing can be seen from another level, like the earth. Say one country is killing another. This is not seen to be good. It is entirely possible that a life form called country will survive, but the life form called the earth is badly injured.

So the right to kill depends upon the viewpoint of the life form we are discussing. If that life form is stable after the killing, for that life form the killing is justified. Exceptions are present, but for the most part, killing of the same species would not be right. However, if a system is being destabilized, then from the higher-level viewpoint, it is OK to kill.

This would apply to the mental plane as well. Structured thoughts around a particular topic like, say, anger, jealousy, or another negative emotion are also life forms. They need energy and want to grow more and more. Unfortunately, they feed off the energy of other thoughts. From my viewpoint, if my mind contains these negative thoughts, it is bad for my system, and I would kill them. The same action by me would seem to be totally partial to one particular set of thoughts, and I would not be behaving as the impartial god I am supposed to be. However, there is a larger ecosystem that I am trying to protect. In fact, all that "I" think I am made up of, I will try to balance. Thus, if a particular set of thoughts is giving me a headache, I prefer to concentrate on other thoughts. This would automatically mean that the worrisome thoughts would be killed off. Thus, killing is justifiable if the larger system is being maintained. This definition of a larger system is, of course, absolutely arbitrary. If I define my body as myself, I would take steps to save it, but it might be in the process killing other people. Now a set of people may be dying to save the world, and killing a set of people to save the world maybe justifiable. Thus the grouping of living things is arbitrary from higher planes, while each plane is absolutely valid in its own right.

Again, is killing justified? This depends on which plane are we talking about. It is actually a complex question. In general, it is not.

Which actions are correct for preserving the system can be seen only from a higher level. At the same level, one can never decide this answer. Hence, the universal rule through the ages has been that we cannot kill one of the same kind. When things go out of control, as Krishna said, someone (he himself) will come from a higher plane to set right things. We will never be able to understand the logic of killing a set of people and letting another set live. Only he can decide that. This is similar to us deciding which cells in our body we can shave off, or which we can amputate if infected, and so on.

So let us try the question in simpler terms: Is killing justified? Yes, if it keeps the system running, but only a higher-level entity can decide what can be killed on a lower plane. This can never be decided on the same level.

Is It Right to Kill Ourselves?

For this we need to look at ourselves and our cells. Suppose there is a cell in the brain or in an eye. I require it in order to function. Naturally, I have caused it a great deal of stress. If the cell decides to give up because of the stress, I will have a huge problem! Yes, I understand it is not sustainable to stress only one or a few cells, but I need them at that time. In fact, I have spent a lot of time and energy to get the cell at that place and time. To lose it at this crucial juncture would be a problem for me. This is similar to a warrior during war, or a sportsman when he is required to act. At that time, if the person decides to quit, or take his or her own life, that action would waste the work of the entire system. To get a replacement and recreate the scenario would take a long time and a great effort and may not even be possible.

This is similar to us being in God's system and being stressed. Please refer to the earlier section in which we learn that we must invoke God and act accordingly. However, at no point should we give up and do nothing – or kill ourselves.

Additionally, there are huge universes on a plane lower than the plane we are on. Our organs depend on us maintaining ourselves in equilibrium. In turn, their cells depend on the organs, and we have learned that there are levels even below the cellular level. By suicide, all these levels will also be annihilated. Does this matter? Of course it does. Imagine if the sun were to give up due to a reason we don't understand. Would that not be the end of our entire properly running solar system? Does all this matter to the higher levels? That depends upon the criticality of that cell, organ, or person. However, we don't want our cells to voluntarily give up the tasks they were meant to do, and hence we should behave responsibly.

Is the Majority Always Right?

The question I am asking here is a basic tenet of many types of government; for example democracy or dictatorship and so on. It also affects the basic rules used to decide what is right and what is wrong. For example, the rule often used to determine if a certain thing is right or wrong is this: It should be for the greatest good for the greatest number. In other words, if an action is beneficial to most, then that course should be taken. Of course most constitutions prevent excessive misuse of this by declaring some fundamental rights that cannot be usurped by the greatest number; for example, the right to life. But, in general, is majority the right way to go?

The basic flaw with the majority model is that it does not consider a higher level entity as the governing entity at all. For example, I should ideally dictate what my body should be doing right now. Imagine a tiger is chasing me, and all my cells decide to take a vote, and they vote that they should rest, as that is the greatest good for the greatest number. At the cellular and organ level, this is valid. But it is not valid at my level. At my level, I vote that my cells and organs should keep working harder to help me run faster! In general, the cells and organs should work in such a way to keep the equilibrium if the system, realizing that they will never know the full picture, and why they should do what they are being asked to do. In effect this is the basis of *Karma yoga* (Do your duty without worrying about the results). Even if the majority fell that they should not do their allotted work, the right thing for enlightened individuals is to do their work; otherwise the entire system will collapse. If the system collapses, the majority will die in any case.

Unanswered Questions

There are many unanswered questions, and the more we think about it, the longer the list becomes. This book has attempted to answer a few fundamental questions. I have presented my theory in a broad scope. Attempting to provide a more precise understanding will require much more work. As I said before, the law is a broad-based one, and to use it for finer understanding requires elaborate study. Here are some topics I would like to expand upon in the future:

- If we consider earth as one living thing (with its own levels beneath it), what would earth be part of at a higher level? If the earth is like a cell, what are the other cells? Is the earth already interacting with other such systems?

- If we are part of a larger system, are we being observed? Are we being kept healthy by some source that we are not able to see? If we are, what is the role of earth? I am sure it must have a role other than to just exist.

- The earth is a place where the energy of the sun is trapped either in plants directly or in the animals that feed on them. Just as we eat plants, are we part of some garden being grown to be eaten?

- The Vedas mention nine Lokas, or worlds, among which the earth sits in the middle. This is totally understandable as we saw in the previous sections. In that case, what is our dharma to the higher lokas? Are we doing it? The higher planes are absolutely dependent on our well-being and on our loyalty to the system. Are we living our part?

- If there are lokas below our loka (not physically, but in a logical way maybe), how do we ensure everything is going on properly there? What are the lower lokas looking to us for?

- Can the field of medicine benefit from all this theory? If cancer is a set of cells deciding they have had enough of the system they are in, and they want out, the parallel is a state that wants to separate from the country. How we solve the problem in the country could indicate how we cure cancer.

- Which is better, socialism or capitalism?

Bibliography

1. Geoffrey Hodson. Meditations on the Occult Life. The Theosophical publishing house, Adyar, second edition 1986.

2. Pandit Rajmani Tigunait Ph.D. From Death to Birth. The Himalayan Institute Press Honesdale, Pennsylvania USA. ISBN 0-89389-14

CPSIA information can be obtained
at www.ICGtesting.com
Printed in the USA
BVHW06s0941090818
523884BV00009B/133/P